Basic
Italian

Course Book

Berlitz Publishing
New York   London   Singapore

Contacting the Editors
Every effort has been made to provide accurate information in this publication, but changes are inevitable. The publisher cannot be responsible for any resulting loss, inconvenience or injury. We would appreciate it if readers would call our attention to any errors or outdated information. We also welcome your suggestions. Please contact us at: comments@berlitzpublishing.com

Cover and pack redesign © April 2012
Printed in China

Publishing Director: Mina Patria
Commissiong Editor: Kate Drynan
Editorial Assistant: Sophie Cooper
Audio Producer: Paul Ruben Studio
Text: Anna Di Stefano, Margaret Powell, Daniela Trevari Gennari
Cover Design: Beverley Speight
Interior Design: Max Crandall
Production Manager: Raj Trivedi
Opener Illustrations: Andy Levine
Illustrations: David Chen, Lyndall Culbertson, Mona Daly, Daniel Dumont, Annie Gusman, Fanny Mellet Berry, Dan Potash, Chris Reed,George Thompson, Kurt Vargo
Maps: MAGELLAN Geographix, Parrot Graphics

Contents

Unit **1** is about getting to know people. When you have completed this unit, you will know how to:

- exchange greetings
- introduce yourself and others
- ask for and give information about names, nationalities, and languages spoken

Presentazioni

Word Bank

Benvenuti!	*Welcome!*	il nome	*first name*
Buon giorno!	*Good day!*	parla	*you speak, he/she speaks*
buono/a	*good*		
Mi chiamo…	*My name is…*	qui	*here*
Si chiama…	*Your name is…, His/Her name is…*	russo/a	*Russian*
		signora	*Mrs./Madam*
Come…?	*How…?*	signore/signor	*Mr./Sir*
francese	*French*	spagnolo/a	*Spanish*
giapponese	*Japanese*	Suo	*your, his, her*
inglese	*English*	tedesco/a	*German*
mio	*my*		

Mi chiamo...

Giving and finding out basic information

1.

The hotel receptionist is asking someone's name, nationality, and where she comes from. Listen to the dialogue and repeat it. Practice saying what you hear.

Come si chiama, signora?	What's your name? (to a woman)
Mi chiamo...	My name is...
È italiana?	Are you Italian?
No, sono americana.	No, I'm American.
Di dov'è?	Where are you from?
Ma parla bene italiano.	But you speak Italian well.
Come mai?	How come?
Mio marito è italiano.	My husband is Italian.

2.

Listen to the dialogue again and decide whether the following statements are true or false.

1. Maria Santoni è italiana.

2. Maria parla bene italiano.

3. È di Boston.

3.

Listen to the alphabet and repeat it. Then try spelling the following names.

Carol Hughes   Janet Wilkes   Brian Kelly   Julian Higgins

Listen to the recording to check your pronunciation. Make sure that you are able to spell your own name in Italian.

4. *The hotel receptionist checks a guest's first and last names. Listen to the dialogue and repeat it.*

Il Suo nome?	*Your first name?*
E il cognome?	*And last name?*
Come si scrive?	*How is it spelled?*
Va bene.	*That's fine.*

5. *It's your first day at a language school in Italy and the people in your class are introducing themselves. Listen to the recording and match the names to their nationalities.*

Example: Brigitte Verdier è francese.

Brigitte Verdier	spagnolo/spagnola
Gianni Guerzoni	giapponese
Ernst Giese	francese
Noriko Tosheiba	russo/russa
Maria de Santez	italiano/italiana
Ludmila Gogoleff	tedesco/tedesca

DidYouKnow?

Thanks to radio and television, a standardized Italian has been spoken across Italy for many years. There are twenty dialects in Italy, one for each region. Several of them actually have the status of languages, so Italians quickly recognize someone is not from their region.

6. *How would you ask someone if they spoke the following languages: English, Russian, Spanish, German, French, or Japanese?*

Example: Parla inglese?

Close-up

The endings of words are very important in Italian. When using verbs to express what they are doing, thinking, or feeling, Italians rely on the endings of the verbs to indicate who or what is doing the action. Though the subject pronouns (I, he, she, we, you, and they) exist, they are normally only used for emphasis and you will see examples of this later. In the dictionary, verbs are listed in the infinitive form and most verbs will end in either **-are, -ere,-** *or* **-ire.** *"To speak" is* **parlare.**
Remove **-are** *and add:*

> **-o, parlo** *to mean "I speak."*

> **-a, parla** *to mean either "you speak" or "he/she/it speaks."*

Some verbs have **-si** *on the end of the infinitive form, and are known as reflexive verbs, such as* **chiamarsi,** *which is the equivalent of* **chiamare + si** *and literally means "to call oneself."* **Chiamare** *is treated the same way as* **parlare,** *but* **-si** *changes in the following way:*

With **chiamo**, use **mi**:	**Mi chiamo...**	*I call myself... or I am called...*
With **chiama**, use **si**:	**Si chiama...**	*You are called... or He, she, or it is called...*

Of course some verbs are completely irregular and do not follow a pattern. For example, note the verb **essere,** *meaning "to be":*

> **sono** *I am...*

> **è** *You are... or he, she, it is...*

Adjective endings also are important and often tell whether the person or thing being described is either masculine or feminine. Adjectives ending in **-o** *are masculine and those ending in* **-a** *are feminine. But those ending in* **-e** *can be either masculine or feminine.*

-o = *Masculine*	Paul è americano.
-a = *Feminine*	Maria è americana.
-e = *Masculine or Feminine*	John è inglese. Elizabeth è inglese.

Parlo italiano, ma solo un po'

Talking about how well you speak a language

Word Bank

Italian	English	Italian	English
abbastanza	*quite*	il modulo d'iscrizione	*enrollment form*
benissimo	*very well*	molto	*very*
Buona sera.	*Good afternoon./ Good evening.*	Mosca	*Moscow*
la città	*city*	nessuno/a	*none*
la conoscenza	*knowledge*	non	*not*
elementare	*elementary*	ottimo/a	*excellent*
Grazie.	*Thank you.*	Parigi	*Paris*
il gruppo	*group*	parlato/a	*spoken*
imparare	*to learn*	per	*for*
l'indirizzo	*address*	Perchè?	*Why?*
intensivo	*intensive*	piccolo/a	*small*
lieto/a	*glad*	questo/a	*this*
la lingua	*language*	solo	*only*
il lavoro	*work*	lo straniero	*foreigner*
ma	*but*	svizzero/a	*Swiss*
medio/a	*fair*	. . . , vero?	*. . . , right?*

1. *Mr. Motta is showing a German colleague, Franz Klaus, around town when he meets Mr. Ferrari. Listen as they exchange greetings and Mr. Klaus is introduced. Listen to the dialogue and repeat it.*

Come sta?	*How are you?*
Bene, grazie, e Lei?	*Fine thanks, and you?*
Non c'è male.	*Not bad.*
Questo è il signor Franz Klaus.	*This is Mr. Franz Klaus.*
Piacere./Molto lieto.	*Pleased to meet you.*
È qui in vacanza.	*He is here on vacation.*

IMPARARE
INGLESE, TEDESCO
FRANCESE, SPAGNOLO
ITALIANO PER STRANIERI

Nome _____
Cognome _____
Indirizzo _____
Telefono _____
Nazionalità _____
Numero di passaporto _____

TELEFONA OGGI **Berlitz**®
Via Mercadante, 17MM Loreto ☎ 555 5399
Via Larga, 8MM Duomo ☎ 555 0814

2. *This is part of an application form for an Italian language course, can you fill it in?*

3. *Match the correct answers to the questions in the following lists. When you have done this, cover up the reply column and see if you can supply your own answers. Then cover up the question column and see if you can provide your own questions.*

1. Come sta il signor Motta?   a. Sì, è italiano.

2. Il signor Klaus è svizzero?   b. Sta bene.

3. Il signor Klaus è qui per lavoro?   c. No, è tedesco.

4. Il signor Ferrari è italiano?   d. No, è qui in vacanza.

4. *The hotel receptionist is having difficulty communicating with a young French woman who does not speak Italian. He sees Mrs. Pasini sitting in the lounge and asks her if she speaks French. Listen to the dialogue and repeat it.*

Buona sera.	Good evening.
Sto molto bene.	I'm very well.
Abbastanza bene.	Quite well.
Lei parla francese, vero?	You speak French, don't you?
Parlo un po'...	I speak a little...
Ma non molto bene.	But not very well.
Perchè?	Why?

5. *Match the correct answers to the questions in the following lists. When you have done this, cover up the reply column and see if you can supply your own answers. Then cover up the question column and see if you can provide your own questions.*

1. La signora Pasini parla bene francese?   a. No, è francese.

2. La signorina parla italiano?   b. No, non parla bene francese.

3. La signorina è tedesca?   c. No, non parla italiano.

6. *There are several ways to say how well you do things. Rank these words from very well (4) to not very well (1).*

1. _____ bene

2. _____ abbastanza bene

3. _____ non molto bene

4. _____ molto bene

Did You Know?

You say **Buon giorno** up until 4:30 or 5:00 P.M. and **Buona sera** there after for the rest of the day. **Ciao** is a friendly, informal greeting which can be used at any time of day for either "Hello" or "Good-bye."

7.

Your friends from the language school introduce themselves and assess their own language competence. Use the following table to help you compose sentences.

Example: Mi chiamo Gianni. Sono italiano, di Milano, e parlo francese ma solo un po'.

Nome	Città	Lingua parlata	Conoscenza
Brigitte	Parigi	russo	ma non molto bene
Ernst	Hannover	inglese	abbastanza bene
Noriko	Tokyo	italiano	ma solo un po'
Maria	Madrid	tedesco	abbastanza bene
Ludmila	Mosca	spagnolo	ma non molto bene

Close-up

Stare *actually means "to stay," but it is sometimes used in idiomatic phrases to mean "to be":*

Sto bene.   *I am well.*

If you want to say "I am" use **sono**.

Forms of address

Notice that when Mr. Ferrari addresses Mr. Motta directly he says: **Buon giorno, signor Motta**, *but when Mr. Motta introduces Mr. Klaus he says:* **Questo è il signor Klaus.**

Il *and* **la**, *are two words for (the definite article) "the" in Italian.* **Il** *is used for most masculine nouns, and* **la** *is used for most feminine nouns:* **il signore** *and* **la signora,**

If you do not know the name of the man you are addressing, use **signore: Scusi, signore.**

If you do know his name, say **signor: Scusi, signor Motta.**

To say that someone does not do something, add **non** *before the verb:*

Non parlo italiano.   *I don't speak Italian.*

This can also be used for negative questions:

Non parla italiano?   *Don't you speak Italian?*

If you're checking something, you can use the quick question **vero?**:

Lei parla francese, vero?   *You speak French, right?/don't you?*

Abito a Verona

Talking about where you live

Word Bank

abito	*I live…/I am living…*	Genova	*Genoa*
Mi chiamo …	*My name is …*	mamma	*Mom*
la domanda	*question*	la risposta	*answer*
Dove?	*Where?*	Venezia	*Venice*
Firenze	*Florence*	vicino/a	*near*

RECORDING

1. **Alessandra is a new face at the club that Matteo goes to and he decides to get to know her. They are young and use the informal form of address. Listen to the dialogue and repeat it.**

Come ti chiami?	*What's your name? (informal)*
Non sei di qui, vero?	*You're not from here, are you?*
Abito qui.	*I live here.*
Dove abiti?	*Where do you live?*
Qui vicino.	*Near here.*

2. **Match the answers to the questions in the following lists. When you have done this, cover up the reply column and see if you can supply your own answers. Then cover up the question column and see if you can provide your own questions.**

1. Dove abiti?   a. Mi chiamo Alessandra.

2. Come ti chiami?   b. No, sono di Firenze.

3. Sei di qui?   c. Abito qui vicino.

3. *Ask the appropriate question! You meet a woman and her young nephew at a museum. What questions do you ask each of them to elicit the answers below? Make sure you use the correct form of address for each.*

Signora Manzoni	Filippo
1. Mi chiamo Giulia Manzoni.	Mi chiamo Filippo.
2. Sono di Genova.	No, non sono di qui.
3. Abito a Venezia.	Abito a Verona.
4. Sì, parlo inglese.	No, non parlo inglese.

RECORDING

4. *Now that we are nearing the end of the unit, here are some people saying good-bye to each other. Listen and repeat!*

DidYouKnow?

There are several ways of saying "good-bye." **Arrivederci** *is the most common and can be used in any circumstances. If you wish to be very formal when saying good-bye to one person whether male or female, you should say* **ArrivederLa.**

Buona notte *is used last thing at night.*

5. *Listen and write! Listen to the last recording again and choose an appropriate good-bye for each of the situations depicted in the illustrations below. Use the Did You Know? to help you decide.*

1. Arrivederci   2. Buona notte   3. ArrivederLa   4. Ciao

a.

b.

c.

d.

Your turn

You get to know some people at your hotel. Listen to the prompts and repeat your part in the dialogues.

Pronunciation

*The letter **u** is pronounced "oo" in Italian wherever it occurs. Say:*

> Buon giorno   qui   buonanotte   lingua

*The combination **ch** always sounds like "k" and never "ch." Try the following:*

> mi chiamo   Chianti   chilo   perché

*When **c** is followed by **e** or **i** it is pronounced "ch." Try saying:*

> francese   piacere   ciao   arrivederci

*There is no letter "j" in Italian words, except for those borrowed from a foreign language, but whenever **g** is followed by **e** or **i**, it sounds like "j." Try saying:*

> Genova   giapponese   Gianni   Giulia

Listen to the recording to check your pronunciation.

To ask a question in Italian, you simply raise your voice at the end of a sentence. Listen to the five recorded examples and decide whether they are questions or answers.

Close-up

There are two ways of addressing someone in Italian, one formal and one informal. You use the formal when talking to an acquaintance or colleague and the informal when talking to a member of the family, a young person, or a friend. To obtain the informal "you" from the infinitive **parlare**, drop **-are** and add **-i**, **parli**. For **chiamarsi**, (to be called) in addition change the **si** to **ti**.

	Formal	Informal
Do you speak Italian?	**Parla** italiano?	**Parli** italiano?
What's your name?	Come **si chiama**?	Come **ti chiami**?

To say "How about you," you will also have to remember that there is a formal form, **E Lei?** and an informal form, **E tu?**

Sei is the informal form of "you are."

Checkpoints

Use the checklist to test what you've learned in this unit and review anything you're not sure of.

Can you . . . ?

	Yes	No
• *greet people* . . . . Buon giorno. / Buona sera.	❑	❑
• *say good-bye* . . . . Arrivederci. / Ciao.	❑	❑
• *ask someone's name* . . . . Come si chiama?/Come ti chiami?	❑	❑
• *give your own name* . . . . Mi chiamo . . .	❑	❑
• *ask where someone is from* . . . . Di dov'è? /Di dove sei?	❑	❑
• *say where you are from* . . . . Sono di . . .	❑	❑
• *ask where someone lives* . . . . Dove abita? / Dove abiti?	❑	❑
• *say where you live* . . . . Abito a . . .	❑	❑
• *give your nationality* . . . . Sono americano del Nord. / Sono americana del Nord.	❑	❑
• *ask if someone speaks English* . . . . Parla inglese? / Parli inglese?	❑	❑
• *say you speak only a little Italian* . . . . Parlo italiano, ma solo un po'.	❑	❑
• *introduce someone* . . . . Questo è . . . / Questa è . . .	❑	❑
• *say pleased to meet you* . . . . Piacere. / Molto lieto. / Molto lieta.	❑	❑
• *ask how someone is* . . . . Come sta? / Come stai?	❑	❑

- *say how you are feeling* . . . . ❑ . . . . . ❑
  Sto molto bene. / Non c'è male.

- *say "Thank you"* . . . . ❑ . . . . . ❑
  Grazie.

- *ask how something is written/spelled* . . . . ❑ . . . . . ❑
  Come si scrive?

- *spell your name in Italian* . . . . ❑ . . . . . ❑

Learning tips

Find the best time of day to do your studying and always try to do it at that time. Short regular periods of study are more effective than one long session at weekly intervals.

Aim to complete one section at each session. Make sure you understand everything by reading all the notes and referring when necessary to the Learner's Guide.

Make sure that you remember how to pronounce **ci, ce, ch, ge, gh,** *and* **gi** *by highlighting them in your book.*

Do you want to learn more?

Do you have access to Italian-language newspapers or magazines? If so, turn to the foreign news section, and see how many country names you are able to recognize. If you don't have access to Italian-language publications, the Italian Consulates or the National Tourist Office may be able to help you.

Unit 2 concentrates on talking about what you do. When you have completed the unit, you will be able to:

- talk about your job and say how long you have been doing it

- talk about what you do if you are not employed

- talk about where you work

Faccio l'insegnante 2

Word Bank

Italian	English	Italian	English
l'anno	*year*	lavoro	*I work*
l'avvocato	*lawyer*	il lavoro	*work/job*
la ditta	*firm*	lavora	*you work, he/she works*
fa	*you do, he/she does*	il meccanico	*mechanic*
faccio	*I do*	il medico	*doctor*
il giorno	*day*	il mese	*month*
l'idraulico	*plumber*	la parrucchiera/ il parruchiere	*hairstylist*
l'impiegato	*office worker*	la ragioniera (f.)	*accountant*
l'infermiere/a	*nurse*	lo scultore	*sculptor*
l'ingegnere (m.)	*engineer*	la settimana	*week*
l'insegnante (m. o f.)	*high school schoolteacher*	lo studente/la studentessa	*student*
interessante	*interesting*	studia	*you study, he/she studies*

Che lavoro fa?

Talking about jobs

RECORDING

1. ***Max Newman is North American and works as an engineer for the Fiat company. Listen and repeat.***

Sono qui per lavoro.	*I am here for work.*
Che lavoro fa?	*What do you do?*
Faccio l'ingegnere.	*I'm an engineer.*
Da quanto tempo?	*For how long?*
È interessante?	*Is it interesting?*

2. ***Find the correct reply for the questions below. When you have done this, cover up the reply column and see if you can supply your own answers. Then cover up the question column and see if you can provide your own questions.***

1. Che lavoro fa il signore?	a. No, lavora per la Fiat.
2. Lavora per la Ford?	b. Da dieci anni.
3. Da quanto tempo lavora per questa ditta?	c. Sì, molto.
4. È interessante il suo lavoro?	d. Fa l'ingegnere.

RECORDING

3. ***Listen to the numbers 1–20 several times and repeat them in the pauses provided.***

Without looking, listen to each number again and try saying the number which follows before listening to it.

1	uno	8	otto	15	quindici
2	due	9	nove	16	sedici
3	tre	10	dieci	17	diciassette
4	quattro	11	undici	18	diciotto
5	cinque	12	dodici	19	diciannove
6	sei	13	tredici	20	venti
7	sette	14	quattordici		

4. *Listen to these people talking about how long they have been doing things and then answer the questions below.*

Example: Da quanto tempo abita qui? Da un mese.

1. Il signore studia tedesco da quattro anni?

2. La signorina è in vacanza da una settimana?

3. La signora è a Roma da tre giorni?

4. Il signore non sta bene da un giorno?

5. *Listen and choose! Number the jobs illustrated below in the order in which you hear them. Watch out: Not all jobs mentioned are illustrated.*

_____ **meccanico**   _____ **infermiera**   _____ **insegnante**

_____ **studente**   _____ **medico**   _____ **parrucchiera**

6.   *Listen to the recording once again and decide whether you would use **il**, **l'**, **lo**, or **la** as the word for "the" (the definite article) for each profession listed.*

Your turn

You meet a colleague on a business trip and get to know a little about her. Listen to the prompts on the recording then write down the details about the person in your diary.

Close-up

In the Italian language, all nouns are either masculine or feminine. Generally, nouns ending in **-o** are masculine, nouns ending in **-a** are feminine, and those ending in **-e** are either masculine or feminine. It is important to note that the words for the indefinite article "the" **(il, lo, l',** and **la)** change accordingly:

Masculine	Feminine
il meccanico	**la** parrucchiera
lo studente	**l'**infermiera
l'ingegnere	**l'**insegnante

Use **lo** in front of masculine words beginning with **s** plus another consonant or **z: lo** studente.

Notice that **lo** and **la** become **l'** when they occur in front of a vowel: **l'**ingegnere, **l'**insegnante.

Corporations, companies, and large businesses are always feminine, such as **la Ford.**

Per lavoro means "for work," and the word **lavoro** is used as a noun. **Lavoro per...** means "I work for," and **lavoro** is used in its verb form, **lavorare,** which means "to work."

When people talk about their jobs or work, they often use **faccio** which literally means "I do":

Faccio il meccanico.   **Faccio la** parrucchiera.
Faccio l'ingegnere.   **Faccio lo** scultore.

Da can mean many things. In the conversations and dialogues you have heard, **da** is used to refer to how long someone has been doing something up to the present time:

Abito qui **da** tre mesi.   I've been living here for three months.

Sono studente

Talking about other kinds of work

W o r d   B a n k

aiuta	*helps*	l'impresa	*business*
amore mio	*my love*	innamorato/a	*in love*
la casalinga	*housewife*	in proprio	*self-employed*
cercare	*to look for*	io	*I*
conquistare	*to conquer*	Mi dispiace.	*I'm sorry.*
il corso	*course*	per	*for, in order to*
il cuore	*heart*	perché	*because*
disoccupato/a	*unemployed*	il poeta	*poet*
disperatamente	*desperately*	lo scopo della visita	*objective of the visit*
in esilio	*in exile*	sempre	*always, still*
l'esperienza	*experience*	la storia dell'arte	*art history*
faticoso	*tiring*	tanto	*so much, so long*
ho	*I have*	tesoro	*darling*
imparare	*to learn*	trovare	*to find*

1. *Mr. Martinelli is retired. and he and his wife have been on vacation for four weeks. Mr. Bellini is not so fortunate. He runs his own business and finds it hard work. Listen and repeat the dialogue.*

È da tanto.	*It's a long time.*
Sì, lo so.	*Yes, I know.*
Sono in pensione.	*I'm retired.*
Mia moglie lavora sempre.	*My wife is always working.*
Perché sono casalinga.	*Because I am a housewife.*
Lavoro in proprio.	*I am self-employed.*
Ho una piccola impresa.	*I have a small business.*

2. *Choose and write the correct answer from the alternatives given.*

1. Il signor Martinelli è in vacanza da quattro settimane perché
   a. è insegnante.
   b. è in pensione.

2. Sua moglie lavora sempre perché
   a. è infermiera.
   b. è casalinga.

3. Il signor Bellini trova il suo lavoro molto faticoso perché
   a. lavora in proprio.
   b. è avvocato.

RECORDING

3. *Giorgio is unemployed. He meets up with Paul in a bar in Siena. Paul is studying Italian and Art History. Listen to their conversation and repeat what they say.*

Che lavoro fai?	What type of work do you do?
Purtroppo sono disoccupato.	Unfortunately, I am unemployed.
Sono qui per cercare lavoro.	I'm here to look for a job.
Che cosa studi?	What are you studying?
Per quanto tempo stai qui ?	How long are you staying here?

4. *Find the correct reply! When you have done this, cover up the reply column and see if you can supply your own answers. Then cover up the question column and see if you can provide your own questions.*

1. Che lavoro fa Giorgio?   a. È studente.

2. Da quanto tempo?   b. Purtroppo è disoccupato.

3. Che lavoro fa Paul?   c. Studia la storia dell'arte.

4. Che cosa studia?   d. Per sei mesi.

5. Per quanto tempo sta qui?   e. Da nove mesi.

Your turn

Imagine you meet a fellow student in a language course in Siena. Listen to the prompts on the recording and repeat your part.

5. *Listen to the following people and then fill in the table below. The first one is done for you.*

	Lavoro	Esperienza	Scopo della visita	Per quanto tempo
Paul	studente	3 anni	per imparare italiano	un mese
Fabrizio				
Anna Maria				

6. *Match the two columns! In the first column, you will read about a series of life situations. What would you do in each situation? Select the appropriate sentence from the second column.*

1. Sono disoccupata.

2. Sono inglese, abito in Italia da una settimana e non parlo italiano.

3. Mia moglie è in vacanza con un medico francese!

4. Sono in pensione e cerco un corso interessante.

a. Sono qui per studiare la storia dell'arte.

b. Sono qui per cercare lavoro.

c. Sono qui per parlare con l'avvocato.

d. Sono qui per imparare l' italiano.

Close up

Per *is used to talk about a period of time starting from the present:*

Per quanto tempo stai qui?   *How long are you staying here?*

Sto qui **per** un anno.   *I am staying here for one year.*

If you want to say how long you have already been doing something, use **da.**

Studio italiano **da** tre anni.   *I've been studying Italian for three years.*

Notice that **per** *can also mean "in order to":*

Sono qui **per** lavorare.   *I am here (in order) to work.*

Lavoro in un ospedale

Talking about where you work

Word Bank

l'agenzia	agency	moltissimo	very much
l'ambulatorio veterinario	veterinarian's office	il negoziante	shopkeeper
animali piccoli	small animals	il negozio	shop
l'architetto	architect	noioso/a	boring
articoli sportivi	sport's equipment	nuovo/a	new
l'autofficina	vehicle workshop	il personale	staff
la banca	bank	Le piace?	Do you like? (formal)
bello/a	beautiful	Mi piace...	I like...
il custode	security guard	prodotti omeopatici	homeopathic products
la fabbrica	factory	piuttosto	rather
la farmacia	drugstore	simpatico/a	friendly
il/la farmacista	pharmacist	lo studio medico	doctor's office

1. *Mrs. Peroni is a hairdresser, who owns her own shop, and loves her work because it is creative. However, Mr. Peroni is a security guard in a factory and finds his job boring. Listen and repeat what they say.*

2. *Find the correct reply for the questions below.*

1. Che lavoro fa la signora?
2. È noioso?
3. Che lavoro fa il signore?
4. Dove lavora?
5. È un lavoro interessante?

a. No, è creativo.
b. Fa il custode.
c. In una fabbrica.
d. Fa la parrucchiera.
e. No, è piuttosto noioso.

RECORDING

3. *Listen to the people talking about where they work and match the people to the following advertisements. The first one is done for you.*

MECCANICO
GIORGIO TRATELLI
VIA SICILIANI, 24-TEL. (0583) 55.57.41

a. ____1____

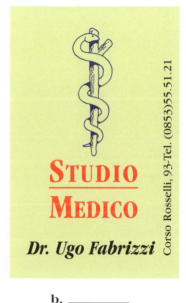

STUDIO
MEDICO
Dr. Ugo Fabrizzi

Corso Rosselli, 93-Tel. (0853)55.51.21

b. _____

Eurofarmacia
Via Fillungio, 26
Tel. (0583) 55533

c. _____

SUGAR
ABBIGLIAMENTO DONNA
ESCLUSIVE: GIORGIO KAUTEN
TOY GIRL - MIRELLA MORI
via Vittorio Veneto, 43
Tel. (0583) 555512

d. _____

Ambulatorio
Dr. Lucia Virgiliano

Piazza Braglia, 21A • Tel. (0858) 55.59.45

e. _____

4. *Read! Everything is going well for Dr. Lo Monaco at the moment.*

Lavora per una ditta dinamica. Il personale è molto simpatico. Il lavoro è interessante. Abita a Siena da un mese. È una città molto bella.

A colleague asks him how he is getting on. How will he reply?

Example: Le piace la nuova ditta?   Sì, mi piace molto. È dinamica.

1. Le piace il personale?

2. Le piace il lavoro?

3. Le piace la città?

5. *Write! Look at the advertisements in Activity 3. If you met these people, what questions might you ask to elicit as much information as possible? The questions should include: What is your name? What type of work do you do? Where do you work? Write the questions down on paper. How do you think they would answer them?*

Pronunciation

1. *In Italian the stress normally falls on the last syllable, for example:* **interessante, ingegnere.** *Practice saying some of the words you have learned:*

l'impiegata   l'avvocato   l'insegnante   lo studente

americano   faticoso   settimana   vacanza

Now listen to the recording to check that you are saying them correctly.

2. *Listen to the recording and try pronouncing the following words. Note where the stress falls:*

esperienza   pensione   ragioniera   parrucchiera

What about the many words that do not follow this rule? Here are a few that you have come across. Do you remember how to say them?

medico   meccanico   università   città   quattordici

Check your pronunciation against the recording.

Close up

In this section you have learned an alternative way of saying what type of work you do, for example: **sono medico.** *This is an easy way to say it because you don't have to use the definite articles* **il, l', lo,** *or* **la.**

When talking about where someone works, you have to use the indefinite article, which is the word for "a" or "an." Italian has four alternative indefinite articles: **un, uno, una,** and **un'. Un** is used with a masculine noun whether or not it begins with a vowel, while **uno** is used with a masculine noun beginning with **s** plus another consonant or **z. Una** is used with a feminine noun and **un'** is used with a feminine noun beginning with a vowel.

Masculine	Feminine
un negozio	**una** banca
un ambulatorio	**un'** autofficina
uno studio	

To ask if someone likes something, say:

Le piace...?   *Do you like...?*

This literally means "is it pleasing" **(piace)** "to you" **(Le).** *You use this when formally addressing someone.*

If you want to say "I like something," you would say **mi piace** which means "it is pleasing" **(piace)** "to me" **(mi).**

Did You Know?

You normally address professional people by their professional title, for example: **Buon giorno, architetto** or **Buona sera, ingegnere.** If you are not sure of their title use **dottoressa,** or **dottore** as a term of respect. Though feminine forms exist for some professions and are used, such as, **dottoressa,** it is quite common to use the masculine form when addressing a woman. In legal circles, especially, it is common to use **avvocato** rather than the rarely used **avvocatessa.**

Checkpoints

- ***ask what type of work someone does*** . . . . ❑ . . . . . ❑
  Che lavoro fa?
  Che lavoro fai?

- ***tell someone what type of work you do*** . . . . ❑ . . . . . ❑
  Faccio l'ingegnere.
  Sono ingegnere.
  Lavoro in proprio.
  Ho una piccola impresa.
  Sono parrucchiera.

- ***ask someone how long they have worked at their job*** . . . . ❑ . . . . . . ❑
  Da quanto tempo lavora per questa ditta?

- ***say how long you have worked at your job*** . . . . ❑ . . . . . ❑
  Da dieci anni.

- ***say if you are retired or unemployed*** . . . . ❑ . . . . . ❑
  Sono in pensione.
  Sono disoccupato/a.

- ***explain reasons for working or studying*** . . . . ❑ . . . . . ❑
  Sono qui per lavoro.
  Sono qui per imparare l'italiano.

- ***say something about your job*** . . . . ❑ . . . . . ❑
  Mi piace molto.
  È interessante.
  È noioso.

- ***say where you work*** . . . . ❑ . . . . . ❑
  Lavoro in un negozio a Montale.
  Lavoro in una farmacia.
  Ho uno studio medico.
  Lavoro in una banca.

- ***address professional people*** . . . . ❑ . . . . . ❑
  Buon giorno, avvocato.

Learning tips

It would be useful to make a note of any irregular stress patterns by underlining them as you go through the book. This would also help you to concentrate on your intonation when you are repeating the dialogues.

Do you want to learn more?

If you keep making the same mistakes in Italian, try to understand why you are doing so. For extra help, refer to the Learner's Guide.

- talk about your family
- talk about whether you are single, married, divorced, widowed, or living with someone
- describe family and friends

La famiglia e gli amici

3

Word Bank

aspetta un bambino	*expecting a baby*	il maschio	*male*
celibe	*single (man)*	morto	*dead*
Chi?	*Who?*	il nipote	*grandson/nephew*
che	*who, whom, which*	la nipote	*granddaughter/niece*
il cugino, la cugina	*cousin*	il nonno	*grandfather*
divorziato/a	*divorced*	la nonna	*grandmother*
da parte di mia madre	*on my mother's side*	nubile	*single (woman)*
la famiglia	*family*	il padre	*father*
la femmina	*female*	più grande	*older/taller/bigger*
la figlia	*daughter*	più piccolo/a	*younger, smaller*
il figlio	*son*	Quanto?	*How much?*
il fratello	*brother*	Quanti?/Quante?	*How many?*
ha	*you have (formal), he, she, or it has*	la sorella	*sister*
hai	*you have (informal)*	il vedovo	*widower*
hanno	*they have*	la vedova	*widow*
immagino	*I imagine*	la zia	*aunt*
la madre	*mother*	lo zio	*uncle*

Sono sposato e ho un figlio

Talking about your family

1.

Mr. Antonelli is divorced and Mrs. Musi is a widow. Listen to them chatting about their families.

Lei è sposato?	*Are you married?*
Sono divorziato.	*I'm divorced.*
Ha figli?	*Do you have children?*
Ho un figlio.	*I have one son.*

When Italians wish to specify the gender of a child, instead of using the words for "son," figlio and "daughter," figlia, they are likely to use un maschio for a male or una femmina for a female!

RECORDING

2.

Fill in the blanks with the missing information based on the dialogue you have just heard.

Il signor Antonelli	La signora Musi
Example: non è sposato	non è sposata
1. _____	non è divorziata
2. _____	è vedova
3. ha un figlio	_____

3.

Check (√) your marital status.

nubile _____   celibe _____   sposato/a _____ divorziato/a _____ vedovo/a _____

RECORDING

4.

Listen to the numbers 20 through 30 and repeat.

20	venti	21	ventuno	22	ventidue	23	ventitré
24	ventiquattro	25	venticinque	26	ventisei	27	ventisette
28	ventotto	29	ventinove	30	trenta		

Now write out the answers to the following:

Example: 30 – 5 = venticinque

1. 21 + 7 =	2. 29 – 6 =	3. 27 + 2 =	4. 22 + 8 =
5. 28 – 4 =	6. 26 – 4 =	7. 23 – 2 =	8. 25 + 1 =

34   *Italian*

5. *Listen to Francesca talking about her family. Identify the following family members. Write them on the family tree below. The first one has already been done for you.*

madre, padre, nonno, nonna, cugina, fratello, sorella, zio, zia

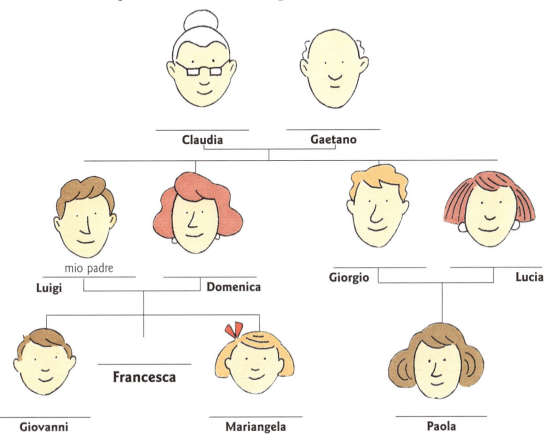

Claudia   Gaetano

mio padre

Luigi   Domenica   Giorgio   Lucia

Francesca

Giovanni   Mariangela   Paola

6. *How are these people related to Francesca? Write down your answers.*

Giorgio, Paola, Lucia, Mariangela
Example: Giorgio è suo zio.

7. *How many? Look again at Francesca's family tree and answer the following questions.*

Example: Quanti figli hanno Gaetano e Claudia?
Gaetano e Claudia hanno due figli: Domenica e Giorgio.

1. Quanti fratelli ha Domenica?

2. Quante sorelle ha Francesca?

3. Quanti nipoti hanno Gaetano e Claudia?

Close up

To say "my," "your," "his," and "her" with a singular noun, you normally use the definite article with the possessive adjective:

My	Your (informal)	Your (formal)/His/Her
il mio avvocato	**il tuo** avvocato	**il suo** avvocato
la mia famiglia	**la tua** famiglia	**la sua** famiglia

But when talking about a close family member in the singular, you drop the definite article:

mio nonno   **tua** zia   **suo** fratello

Note that **suo fratello** can mean "your brother," (formal) "his brother," or "her brother."

Two exceptions to this rule are **mamma** and **papà:**

La mia mamma.   **Il mio** papà.

To ask a friend's age, use the informal:

Quanti anni **hai?**   How old are you? (Literally "How many years do you have?")

To ask someone formally say:

Quanti anni **ha?**   How old is he, she, or it?

Notice how Francesca says she is fifteen:

Ho quindici anni.   I am fifteen. (Literally "I have fifteen years.")

Sono separato e ho una nuova partner

Talking about your marital status

Word Bank

la cognata	*sister-in-law*	lei	*she*
il cognato	*brother-in-law*	lui	*he*
l'ex moglie	*ex-wife*	miei/mie	*my (plural)*
e(d)	*and*	la nuora	*daughter-in-law*
il genero	*son-in-law*	separato/a	*separated*
i genitori	*parents*	la suocera	*mother-in-law*
Lei	*you (formal)*	il suocero	*father-in-law*

1. **Listen to some people talking about their relationships and repeat what they say.**

Io sono separato da due anni.	*I have been separated (from my wife) for two years.*
Ho una nuova partner.	*I have a new partner.*
Sono figlio unico.	*I am an only child.*
Ha una nuova famiglia.	*He has a new family.*

2. *Listen to the recording again and use the words supplied to fill in the blanks in the following sentences.*

1. Io sono _____ da due anni, ma ho una nuova _____.
   Lei ha due _____

2. La mia _____ ha un nuovo _____. Lui ha un
   _____ di diciassette anni.

3. Sono figlio _____. I miei _____ sono _____ ma
   mio padre ha una _____ famiglia.

figli	separato	ex moglie	figlio	partner
unico	marito	genitori	nuova	divorziati

3. *Mario's family situation is exactly the same as Anna's. Can you fill in the missing information for him?*

Anna	Mario
È separata.	_____
Ha un nuovo partner.	_____
Il suo ex marito ha una nuova moglie.	_____
Lui ha una nuova famiglia.	_____

4. *Choose the appropriate word and put the correct article in front of it.*

Example: il nonno + la nonna = i nonni

1. il padre + la madre =

2. il fratello + la sorella =

3. il fratello + il fratello =

4. la sorella + la sorella =

5. il figlio + la figlia =

6. la nipote + la nipote =

7. lo zio + la zia =

8. il cugino + il cugino =

Your turn

You meet a young Italian girl and learn a little about her family. Listen to the prompts and play your part.

5. *You are talking to your friend about his family and acquaintances. Look carefully at the following words and for each one choose the appropriate phrase from the second box.*

Example: il tuo avvocato

padre	genitori
medico	cugina
ragioniera	ex moglie
	sorelle

tuo	i tuoi
il tuo	le tue
la tua	tua

Close up

The last letter of a noun changes when the word is plural and can indicate whether it is masculine plural or feminine plural. The word for "the" (the definite article) will also change accordingly.

Masculine Plural	Feminine Plural
i fratel**li**	**le** sorel**le**
gli ingegner**i**	**le** nipot**i**
gli zi**i**	**le** esperien**ze**

Plural Possessives

	Masculine	Example	Feminine	Example
my	i **miei**	i miei fratelli	le **mie**	le mie sorelle
your (informal)	i **tuoi**	i tuoi fratelli	le **tue**	le tue sorelle
your (formal)/his/her	i **suoi**	i suoi genitori	le **sue**	le sue cugine

Note that i suoi genitori *can mean "your parents," "his parents," or "her parents."*

Subject pronouns are only used for emphasis, as we have seen. They are:

I	**io**		
you (informal)	**tu**	*you (formal)*	**Lei**
she	**lei**	*he*	**lui**

Il marito di Marisa è molto impegnato

Describing your friends

Word Bank

affettuoso/a	*affectionate*	a scuola	*at school*
alto/a	*tall*	sempre	*still, always*
attentamente	*carefully*	sono	*I am…,They are…*
bravo/a	*good*	spesso	*often*
così	*so*	sportivo/a	*sporty*
impegnato/a	*committed, involved*	stanco/a	*tired*
indaffarato/a	*busy*	studioso/a	*studious*
intelligente	*intelligent*	tutto	*all*

1. **Listen carefully! You are in a café and overhear the conversation as an old friend meets up with Marisa and catches up on family news.**

Dimmi!	*Tell me! (informal)*
Com'è?	*What's she like?*
Ti piace, insomma.	*So all in all, you like her.*
Matteo ama sempre lo sport, immagino.	*Matteo still likes sports, I suppose.*
A scuola, sono bravi?	*Do they do well in school?*

2. *Listen again and check off (✓) the following adjectives as you hear them:*

impegnato, indaffarato, stanco, bella, alta, intelligente, affettuosa, simpatica, sportivi, bravi, studiosi.

As you listen to the conversation, list which adjectives apply:

1. *to Marisa's husband*

2. *to Matteo's girlfriend*

3. *to Matteo's friends*

Now look at the lists you have made. What do you notice about the endings of the adjectives in each list?

3. *Complete the sentences below.*

1. Il marito di Marisa è ——————

2. La ragazza di Matteo è ——————

3. I suoi amici sono ——————

4. *Look at the drawings below, and complete the sentences with adjectives from the list provided. Make sure to use the correct endings.*

1. Laura e suo marito sono _____.

2. Rossella è _____.

3. Pino è molto _____.

4. Franco è _____.

impegnato, bello, bravo, intelligente, sportivo, studioso, affettuoso, stanco, contento

Your turn

You are staying with an Italian family as a paying guest while studying at a language school. Listen to the prompts and describe the family to your classmates.

Pronunciation

1. *First try repeating these words after the recording:*

gli   **gli italiani**   **gli ingegneri**
gli studenti   **gli insegnanti**

2. *Here are some sentences for you to get your tongue around:*

a. In generale gli italiani sono bravi ingegneri.
b. Gli studenti sono studiosi se gli insegnanti sono bravi.
c. Gli avvocati sono spesso stanchi perché sono molto impegnati.

3. *And finally* **uno scioglilingua** *– a tongue twister:*

**La moglie del figlio di mia figlia ha otto figli.
Quanti figli in famiglia?**

Close up

In the Italian language, the endings of adjectives change in addition to the article and noun endings:

	Singular	Plural
Masculine:	Giovanni è divorziat**o**.	I miei genitori sono divorziat**i**.
Feminine:	Anna è separat**a**.	Le mie sorelle sono separat**e**.
Masc./Fem.:	Lilia è intelligent**e**.	Le studentesse sono intelligent**i**.
	Paolo è intelligent**e**.	Gli studenti sono intelligent**i**.

If you ask a friend "Do you like?", use the informal **Ti piace?**, *which literally means "Is it pleasing* **(piace)** *to you* **(ti)**?"

Checkpoints

Can you . . . ?   **Yes**   **No**

- *ask if someone is married* . . . . ❑ . . . . . ❑
  Lei è sposato/a?

- *describe your own marital status* . . . . ❑ . . . . . ❑
  Sono sposato/a.
  Sono vedovo/a.
  Sono divorziato/a.
  Sono separato/a.

- *say you have a new partner* . . . . ❑ . . . . . ❑
  Ho un nuovo partner/una nuova partner.

- *ask about someone's family* . . . . ❑ . . . . . ❑
  Ha figli?
  Quanti figli ha?
  Hai fratelli?

- *talk about members of your close family* . . . . ❑ . . . . . ❑
  Ho due figli, un maschio e una femmina.
  Sono figlio unico.
  Ho un fratello ed una sorella.
  I miei genitori sono divorziati.

- *ask someone's age* . . . . ❑ . . . . . ❑
  Quanti anni hai?
  Quanti anni ha?

- *tell how old you are* . . . . ❑ . . . . . ❑
  Ho ventuno anni.

- *describe your family and friends* . . . . ❑ . . . . . ❑
  La ragazza di Matteo è bella.
  Il marito di Marisa è molto impegnato.
  Paolo e il suo papà sono intelligenti.

Learning tips

It is a good idea to go back over past units from time to time. Language learning is a much slower process than many people realize. Do not push yourself. Go over things as often as you need.

Do you want to learn more?

Be selective about the vocabulary you learn. First, learn those items that will be of use to you personally, then read through the rest several times so that the words become part of your passive vocabulary.

Unit 4 is about ordering snacks and drinks, and buying things in shops. When you have completed the unit, you will be able to:

- request and offer something to eat or drink
- accept politely, or refuse, giving an excuse
- ask about prices and buy simple items

Qualcosa da mangiare o da bere?

4

Word Bank

l'aranciata	a carbonated orange drink	l'insalata	salad
Basta.	That's all./ That's enough.	l'insalata russa	Russian salad
		nient'altro	nothing else
bianco	white	il panino	roll, sandwich
il bicchiere	glass	la pasta	pasta, pastry (in a café)
la birra	beer		
il caffè	coffee	la pizzetta	small pizza
la ciambella	doughnut	Prende...	You take..., He/She/It takes...
il cioccolato	chocolate		
il conto	bill	il prosciutto	ham
il cornetto	croissant	la spremuta d'arancia	freshly squeezed orange juice
così	like that		
ecco	here is/ here it is	il tè	tea
il formaggio	cheese	la vaniglia	vanilla
la fragola	strawberry	il vino	wine
il gelato	ice cream	Vorrei...	I would like...
il gusto	flavor	Vuole...	You want/He/She wants...

Vorrei una birra e un panino

Ordering something to eat or drink

1. *A mother and daughter are sitting at an outdoor café and the waiter comes to take their order. How do they order what they want? Listen and repeat what each one orders.*

Che cosa prende?	What will you have?
Vorrei una spremuta d'arancia.	I'd like a freshly squeezed orange juice.
Come vuole il panino?	How would you like your sandwich?
Nient'altro?	Anything else?
Basta così.	That's enough.
Quant'è?	How much is it?

2. *Listen to some people ordering refreshments at a busy café. When you hear someone order any of the items listed on the menu write down how many they order.*

Desidera?	What would you like?
Prego, signora?	Yes, madam?/Can I help you?
Che gusto?	What flavor?

AL BAR

birra	€1,80
whisky	€2,50
martini	€2,10
gelati	€1,20
aranciata	€1,50
cappuccino	€1,00
caffè	€0,80
tè	€1,00
coca-cola	€1,50
vino bianco	€1,30
vino rosso	€1,60
paste	€0,70
ciambelle	€0,70
pizzette	€1,00
panini	€1,00

3. *Are you sure how to order different quantities?*
Fill in the blanks in the columns below.

	1	2
1.	una birra	_____
2.	_____	due Coca-Cola®
3.	un'aranciata	_____
4.	_____	due caffè
5.	un gelato	_____
6.	_____	due spremute
7.	una ciambella	_____
8.	_____	due panini

RECORDING

4. *Listen to some waiters asking people for their orders. There are six recorded examples. Which ones might have been directed at you personally? You have to be very quick to pick them up.*

RECORDING

5. *We will have to find out the total of the bill. Before we do that let's have another look at numbers. Let's start with the tens from forty to ninety:*

40	quaranta	50	cinquanta	60	sessanta
70	settanta	80	ottanta	90	novanta

and now the hundreds:

100	cento	200	duecento	300	trecento
400	quattrocento	500	cinquecento	600	seicento
700	settecento	800	ottocento	900	novecento

and the thousands:

1000	mille	2000	duemila
3000	tremila	4000	quattromila

Can you go on?

6.

Listen to the cashier asking you for the amount of your bill. Number the bills in the order in which you hear the amounts.

a. Cassa _____ 2,79   b. Cassa _____ 3,77   c. Cassa _____ 4,75

d. Cassa _____ 1,45   e. Cassa _____ 3,15

Close up

Prendo *means "I take," from the verb* **prendere**. *Verbs which end in* **-ere** *follow a slightly different pattern from those ending in* **-are**. *Drop the* **-ere** *and add the appropriate ending as follows:*

I	*add* **-o**	prendo
you (informal)	*add* **-i**	prendi
you (formal), he/she/it	*add* **-e**	prende

Vuole . . . ? *and* **Desidera . . . ?** *are ways of saying "Would you like . . . ?"* **Vuole** *comes from the irregular verb* **volere**.

Notice that nouns with an accent on the final letter or foreign nouns that end in a consonant, do not change in the plural: **un tè, due tè, un bar,** *and* **due bar.**

With thirty-one and thirty-eight, the final **a** *on* **trenta** *is dropped to give* **trentuno** *and* **trentotto**. *This is because the letter that follows is a vowel. The same rule applies to all the tens:* **quaranta**, **quarantuno**, *and* **quarantotto**.

Vorrei *means "I would like" and you will need to use it often. It can be used with a noun or with a verb:*

Vorrei un gelato.	*I would like an ice cream.*
Vorrei prendere un tè.	*I would like to have a tea.*

Prego *literally means "I pray," and it is used in different circumstances and with differing intonations to mean different things. Here are some of the main uses of* **prego**:

Prego?	*to attract someone's attention when you need them to repeat what was said*
Prego!	*when allowing someone to pass in front of you (in a waiting line)*
	in response to someone saying "Thank you," as we might say "Don't mention it."

Offro io!

Offering something to eat or drink

Word Bank

l'amaro	*a popular, bitter-tasting liqueur*	la pera	*pear*
analcolico	*nonalcoholic*	il pompelmo	*grapefruit*
bere	*to drink*	preferisco	*I prefer*
con	*with*	prendete	*you take (plural)*
il ghiaccio	*ice*	qualcosa	*something*
Ho fame.	*I'm hungry.*	rosso/a	*red*
Ho sete.	*I'm thirsty.*	senza	*without*
il latte	*milk*	il succo di frutta	*fruit juice*
il limone	*lemon*	volentieri	*willingly*
mangiare	*to eat*	vuoi	*you want (informal)*
offro	*I am offering*	lo zucchero	*sugar*

1. **Giuseppe is in a bar with his friends, buying a round of drinks. Finally he asks you what you would like. Decide what drinks you would like to have.**

Offro io.	*I'm paying.*
Che cosa prendete?	*What are you having? (plural)*
Con ghiaccio?	*With ice?*
No, grazie, senza.	*No thanks, without.*
Io preferisco qualcosa di analcolico.	*I'd prefer something nonalcoholic.*
Per me un bicchiere di vino bianco.	*For me a glass of white wine.*

2. *If you were Giuseppe would you remember everything when you had to order the drinks? Write a list of what people want. Then listen to the recording again to check that you remembered everything correctly.*

3. *It's your turn to buy a round of drinks for some Italian friends at your hotel. How will you give your order?*

It's on me. What are you having?

What are you having, Antonietta?

And for you, Paolo?

Listen to the recording to check your answers.

4. *Graziella visits Serena at her home and is offered something to drink and eat. Listen and then repeat what each one says.*

Che cosa vuoi da bere?	*What would you like to drink?*
Ho sete.	*I am thirsty.*
Al latte o al limone?	*With milk or lemon?*
Vuoi qualcosa da mangiare?	*Would you like something to eat?*
No, grazie, non ho fame.	*No, thank you, I'm not hungry.*

5. *You overhear some people offering friends drinks in a bar. Listen to each bit of conversation carefully and check (✓) whether each person is speaking to just one person or to more than one person. Then listen again and check (✓) whether the person in each case is a friend or an acquaintance. The first one is done for you.*

	One	More than one	Friend	Acquaintance
1.	✓		✓	
2.				
3.				
4.				
5.				

Close up

Che cosa prendete? *This means literally "What will you take?" and the ending **-ete** indicates that you are talking to more than one person. Take the **-ere** ending off the verb **prendere**, "to take" and add **-ete** to give the plural form for "you." All regular verbs ending in **-ere** will follow this pattern.*

Preferisco *means "I prefer." The verb "to prefer" is **preferire**. To say "I prefer," drop the **-ire** ending and add **-isco**. Not all verbs ending in **-ire** follow this pattern.*

Vuoi *means "you want" (informal). For more details on this verb consult the Learner's Guide.*

Avete una guida in inglese?

Asking for an item at a store

Word Bank

Avete ...?	*Do you have ...? (plural)*	il francobollo	*stamp*
il Brasile	*Brazil*	la Germania	*Germany*
il Canada	*Canada*	gratuito/a	*free, gratis*
la cartolina	*postcard*	la guida	*guidebook*
la Cina	*China*	il Messico	*Mexico*
Compra...	*You (formal) buy...* *He/She buys...*	una piantina della città	*a street map of the town*
compri	*you buy (informal)*	quello/a	*that, that one*
costa	*it costs*	gli Stati Uniti	*the United States*
costano	*they cost*		

1.

You are at a tourist information center and there are a few things you need to buy. Listen and repeat.

Avete una guida?	*Have you got a guidebook?*
Quanto costa?	*How much does it cost?*
Quanto costano questi poster?	*How much do these posters cost?*
Mi può dare una piantina della città?	*Can you give me a street map?*
Non compri cartoline?	*Aren't you buying postcards?*
Dieci francobolli per gli Stati Uniti.	*Ten stamps for the United States.*

2. *Listen again to the conversation and decide whether the following statements are true or false.*

1. La signora vuole una guida in inglese.

2. Prende un piccolo poster.

3. Compra cinque cartoline.

4. Compra dieci francobolli per la Gran Bretagna.

5. Costa 34 euro in tutto.

3. *There are several ways of asking for things. Listen to these people asking for what they want, and match the number of the sentence with the corresponding illustration. Then look at the illustrations and ask for the various items in as many ways as possible.*

Example: Vorrei un poster.   Mi può dare questo poster?
        Prendo un poster.   Questo poster, per favore.

a. _____   b. _____

c. _____   d. _____

4. *Which would you use to ask the price of the following items:* **Quanto costa?** *or* **Quanto costano?**

Example: le cartoline   Quanto costano le cartoline?

1. la guida   2. i poster   3. i francobolli   4. la piantina

Pronunciation

1. *Longer phrases are sometimes difficult to say, so let's take a look at a few and practice them.*

una spremuta d' arancia; un panino al formaggio; qualcosa di analcolico; un bicchiere di vino bianco; un Martini con ghiaccio; un tè con latte; un tè al latte; una guida in inglese; un francobollo per gli Stati Uniti; una piantina della città

2. *And now let's try this tongue twister:*

Cinque bicchieri di vino bianco con cinque gelati al cioccolato costano 15 euro.

Close-up

When you want to ask the price of something, remember to think about whether there are one or more items:

Quanto costa?	How much does it cost?	(for one item)
Quanto costano?	How much do they cost?	(for more than one item)
Mi può dare...	Is a polite expression meaning "Can you give me..."	

Notice how the names of countries are said:

gli Stati Uniti	the United States
la Gran Bretagna	Great Britain
il Messico	Mexico

Don't forget that in Italian you must use the definite article "the" with the name of a country.

Checkpoints

Can you . . . ?   **Yes**   **No**

- *say what you would like* . . . . ❑ . . . . . ❑
  Vorrei un panino al formaggio.
  Prendo un bicchiere di vino bianco.

- *say how you would like it* . . . . ❑ . . . . . ❑
  Con ghiaccio.

- *say that that is enough* . . . . ❑ . . . . . ❑
  Basta così.

- *ask how much something costs* . . . . ❑ . . . . . ❑
  Quant'è?
  Quanto costa?
  Quanto costano?

- *say "the drinks are on me"* . . . . ❑ . . . . . ❑
  Offro io.

- *offer drinks to others* . . . . ❑ . . . . . ❑
  Che cosa prende?
  Che cosa prendete?
  Che cosa vuoi da bere?

- *understand prices* . . . . ❑ . . . . . ❑
  Cinquanta euro.

- *accept politely* . . . . ❑ . . . . . ❑
  Prendo volentieri un tè.

- *refuse and give a reason* . . . . ❑ . . . . . ❑
  No, grazie, non ho fame.

- *ask for a specific item* . . . . ❑ . . . . . ❑
  Avete una guida in inglese?
  Mi può dare una piantina della città?

- *choose what you want* . . . . ❑ . . . . . ❑
  Prendo quello grande.
  Questo poster, per favore.

Learning tips

When you study verbs, learn the regular pattern. You will find more information in the Grammar section of the Learner's Guide. That way you can apply the rule to other regular verbs you come across or look up the verbs in the dictionary. A small dictionary with a list of irregular verbs is always useful.

Do you want to learn more?

Use your free time to practice what you have learned. When doing chores, try to remember all the things you have covered in your study sessions. Don't worry if committing things to memory seems a long process. It is difficult for most people.

Unit 5 is about finding your way around. You will learn how to:

- ask for and understand simple directions
- attract someone's attention
- ask for clarification or repetition
- ask about opening and closing hours

Direzioni

5

Word Bank

allora	*well*	a piedi	*on foot*
la buca delle lettere	*mailbox*	la posta	*post office, mail*
la cabina telefonica	*telephone booth*	Prego!	*Don't mention it!*
c'è	*there is*	Prenda!	*Take!*
certo	*of course*	primo/a	*first*
il Colosseo	*the Colosseum*	proprio	*just*
continuare	*to continue*	quarto/a	*fourth*
il corso	*boulevard*	il ristorante	*restaurant*
a destra	*on the right*	scusi	*excuse me*
dritto	*straight ahead*	secondo/a	*second*
il duomo	*cathedral*	a sinistra	*on the left*
la fermata (dell'autobus)	*bus stop*	la strada	*street*
la galleria d'arte	*art gallery*	il supermercato	*supermarket*
girare	*to turn*	terzo/a	*third*
lì	*there*	si trova	*it is situated*
lontano	*far*	la via	*street*
il museo	*museum*	il viale	*avenue*
la piazza	*square*		

C'è un buon ristorante qui vicino?

Asking for directions

1. Listen as this man finds out if there is a good restaurant nearby. Then repeat the dialog.

Scusi.	Excuse me.
C'è un buon ristorante qui vicino?	Is there a good restaurant near here?
Ce n'è uno...	There is one...
Dove si trova?	Where is it situated?
Prenda la prima strada a destra.	Take the first street on the right.
È lontano?	Is it far?
Cinque minuti a piedi.	Five minutes on foot.

2. Study the directions given on the street map above. How would you say:

1. *the second on the right?*   4. *the third on the right?*
2. *the first on the left?*   5. *on the right-hand side?*
3. *the fourth on the left?*   6. *on the left-hand side?*

Now listen to the recording to check your answers.

3. *Some people are trying to find out where certain places are located. Listen to the directions and identify the numbered sites on the street plan below.*

la farmacia   il supermercato   la banca
la cabina telefonica   la buca delle lettere

4. *Listen to the people asking the hotel receptionist how to get to various places. In English write down where each person is going.*

5. *Which would you use in the following circumstances:* **dov'è...?** *or* **c'è... qui vicino?**

1. il duomo
2. il museo
3. una farmacia
4. la galleria d'arte
5. un bar
6. un cinema

6. *Reorder these distances from shortest to longest.*

1. è a cinque minuti a piedi
2. è a centocinquanta metri
3. è a dieci minuti in autobus
4. è a trecento chilometri
5. è proprio qui davanti
6. è a trenta minuti in macchina

Close up

ci	*there*
è	*is*
c'è	*there is* (**ci** *becomes* **c'** *before a vowel*)
ne	*of them* (**ne** *becomes* **n'** *before a vowel*)
ce n'è uno	*there is one of them* (**ci** *becomes* **ce** *when followed by* **ne**).

    C'è una farmacia qui vicino?   Sì, **ce n'è una** in Via Garibaldi.

Note the reply because **farmacia** *is feminine, and* **una** *is also feminine.*

Dove? — Where?

Dov'è? *Where is...?* **Dove** *becomes* **dov'** *before a vowel.*

Dove si trova *is an alternative way of asking where a specific place is located.*

    Dove si trova il museo?

Per andare a Taormina?

Giving information about places in the city

W o r d   B a n k

accanto a	*next to*	partire	*to leave*
andare	*to go*	passare	*to spend*
andiamo	*we are going*	più	*more*
Buon viaggio!	*Have a good journey!*	poi	*then*
davanti a	*in front*	il pomeriggio	*afternoon*
dietro	*behind*	prenotare	*to book*
di fronte a	*opposite*	presto	*early*
dopo	*after*	Può...?	*Can you...?*
facile	*easy*	Quando...?	*When...?*
il Foro Romano	*the Roman Forum*	ripetere	*to repeat*
grazie mille	*many thanks*	San Pietro	*Saint Peter*
l'incrocio	*crossroads*	segnalato/a	*signposted*
indietro	*back*	il semaforo	*traffic lights*
in fondo a	*at the end of*	la tomba	*tomb*
invece	*on the other hand*	l'ufficio degli scavi	*archaeological excavations' office*
lentamente	*slowly*	vado	*I am going, I go*
la mattina	*morning, in the morning*	la visita	*visit*

1.   ***A young woman has rented a car and is traveling to see the famous Greco-Roman theater at Taormina, but unfortunately she has become lost.***

Per andare a Taormina?	*How do I get to Taormina?*
Ha sbagliato strada.	*You've got the wrong road.*
Torni indietro.	*Go back.*
Giri a destra.	*Turn right.*
Può ripetere più lentamente?	*Can you say it again more slowly?*
La strada per Taormina è segnalata.	*The road for Taormina is signposted.*

2. *You just can't get anything right today!*
How would you say you've got these things wrong:

Example: I've got the wrong name! Ho sbagliato nome.

1. *I've got the wrong street!*

2. *I've got the wrong square!*

3. *I've got the wrong town!*

4. *I've got the wrong number!*

5. *I've got the wrong hotel!*

Better luck tomorrow!

RECORDING

3. Listen to the recorded commands and write them down in English.

RECORDING

4. Listen to some people getting information from the hotel receptionist about where things are located. Repeat the conversation.

Dove andate oggi?	*Where are you (plural) going today?*
C'è un autobus?	*Is there a bus?*
La fermata è di fronte all'albergo.	*The bus stop is opposite the hotel.*
È proprio qui dietro l'albergo.	*It's just here, behind the hotel.*
Io parto, purtroppo.	*Unfortunately, I'm leaving.*

DidYouKnow?

It was only after the unification of Italy in the 1860s that the Italian language, based on the Tuscan dialect, emerged as the national language of Italy. Until then, people spoke in their own regional dialects which are still much in evidence today. Despite the fact that Italian was taught in schools, it was only with the onset of radio and television that more and more people began to speak it. Like all languages it is continually changing, and you will find that people have a tendency to simplify things. For example, you will often hear **"davanti l'albergo"** *instead of* **"davanti all'albergo."**

5. *Look at the map below and complete the following sentences using the words supplied to explain exactly where the different buildings are located.*

dietro   davanti   accanto   di fronte   in fondo

1. Il museo è _____.

2. La fermata è _____.

3. La galleria d'arte è _____.

4. La posta è _____.

5. I negozi principali sono

_____.

6. *An Italian friend has planned a day out in Rome for both of you tomorrow and leaves you a note at your hotel to remind you. Fill in the blanks with the appropriate form of* **a: al, all', alla.**

Domani andiamo a Roma, va bene? Arriviamo ___ stazione Termini e da lì prendiamo la metropolitana per andare ___ Colosseo. Poi per andare ___ Foro Romano non è lontano. Il pomeriggio, andiamo ___ Basilica di San Pietro. Passiamo tutto il pomeriggio lì perché è molto interessante. Dopo, andiamo ___ ufficio degli scavi che si trova al Vaticano per prenotare una visita ___ tomba di San Pietro. A domani. Ciao, Ina.

7. *Supply the correct form of "we" of the verb given in parentheses:*

Example: (andare) a Pisa oggi.   Andiamo a Pisa oggi.

1. (preferire) la birra tedesca.

2. La mattina presto (prendere) un caffè.

3. Quando (arrivare) alla Stazione Termini?

4. (visitare) la Basilica di San Pietro questo pomeriggio.

Close up

Torni, giri, continui, *and* **prenda,** *are all formal commands. For the moment all you have to do is to recognize what they mean and that is quite simple.*

Può *means "you can" or "can you?" (formal) and it can be used with any verb you find in the dictionary.*

> **Può** ripetere?   Can you repeat?

A *means "to," "at," or "in":*

> Vado **a** Roma.   *I'm going to Rome.*
>
> Resto **a** casa.   *I'm staying at home.*
>
> Abito **a** Milano.   *I live in Milan.*

Let's look at how you say "to the" or "at the."

> **a + il = al**   **al** Foro Romano
>
> **a + l' = all'**   **all'**incrocio
>
> **a + la = alla**   **alla** Basilica di San Pietro

The following phrases are all used with the Italian preposition **a** *and change in the same way:*

davanti a	*in front of*	davanti **all'**albergo
di fronte a	*opposite*	di fronte **all'**ufficio postale
in fondo a	*at the end of*	in fondo **alla** strada
accanto a	*next to*	accanto **al** cinema
dietro a	*behind*	dietro **alla** stazione

You will probably hear people say **"davanti l'albergo"** *in colloquial use. Note however that "to/into the center" is* **in centro.**

> **andare** *to go*   **vado** *I go*   **andate** *you (plural) go*

If you drop the last three letters of most verbs ending in **-are** *and add* **-ate***, this is the form you will use when talking to more than one person:*

> arriv**are** arriv + **ate**   arriv**ate** *you (plural) arrive*

Andiamo *means "we go" or "we are going." To use "we" with a verb, drop the last three letters and add* **-iamo***:*

> compr**are**, compr**iamo** prend**ere**, prend**iamo** prefer**ire**, prefer**iamo**

Signori *is used to formally address two or more people, so it takes the third person plural form of* **vanno.**

> **Signori,** dove **vanno**?

A che ora apre?

Asking about opening and closing hours

Word Bank

aperto/a	*open*	giorni festivi	*public holidays including Sunday*
aprire	*to open*	Meno male!	*Thank goodness!*
Che peccato!	*What a pity!*	però	*however*
chiudere	*to close*	possibile	*possible*
chiuso/a	*closed*	quasi	*almost*
fare spese	*to shop*	la stagione	*season*
giorni feriali	*working days*		

1. *Two friends meet for a visit around Rome. Repeat what each one says.*

Chiude alle quattordici in questa stagione. — *It closes at 2:00 P.M. this time of year.*

Che peccato! — *What a pity!*
C'è tanto da vedere. — *There's so much to see.*
Meno male! — *Thank goodness for that!*

2. *Listen to the dialogue again and answer the questions.*

1. Perché non è possibile andare al Vaticano questo pomeriggio?

2. Quasi tutti i musei sono chiusi il pomeriggio?

3. A che ora aprono i negozi?

4. A che ora chiudono?

5. Sono aperti tutto il giorno?

RECORDING

3.

Listen to the recorded messages about opening and closing times and write down the information.

	la mattina	**la sera**
	apre	chiude
il museo		
la galleria		
il negozio		
la banca		

RECORDING

4.

Listen to the recording and repeat the days of the week starting with Monday:

lunedì, martedì, mercoledì, giovedì, venerdì, sabato, domenica

5.

Alberto is in Rome on business for an entire week. He is trying to fit as many activities as he can into his schedule. Help him out by organizing his **tempo libero** *(free time). He is free every day from 12:00 P.M. to 2:00 P.M., 4:00 P.M. to 5:00 P.M., and 8:00 P.M. to 11:00 P.M. On Sunday, he is free the entire day. (Note that Italian uses a comma instead of a colon to separate the hours from the minutes). The first one is already done for you.*

Attività possibili: a San Pietro, al Colosseo, a Fontana di Trevi, a fare spese, in discoteca, a villa Borghese, al museo Borghese, etc.

1. lunedì dalle 12,00 alle 2,00 al ristorante "Da Gigi"

_____ _____ _____

2. _____ _____ _____

3. _____ _____ _____

4. _____ _____ _____

5. _____ _____ _____

6. _____ _____ _____

7. _____ _____ _____

Pronunciation

1. *Repeat these double vowel sounds.*

può; più; vuole; vuoi; autobus; Paolo; Pietro; questo;
quattordici; quarto; cinque; farmacia; pronuncia;
piazza; museo

2. *Listen to the following sentences and then repeat them.*

1. Questo autobus va in Piazza San Paolo dove
   c'è una farmacia.
2. Può ripetere più lentamente per piacere?

Close-up

Look at how you use a verb with "they."

For verbs ending in **-ere** *and for many verbs ending in* **-ire** *you drop the last three letters of the verb and add the ending* **-ono.**

Chiud**ono**...	*They close...*
Apr**ono**...	*They open...*

For verbs ending in **-are** *drop the last three letters and add* **-ano.**

Arriv**ano**...	*They arrive...*

If a shop closes at one, you say **"chiude alle tredici,"** *but if it is closed from one to four, you say* **"è chiuso dalle tredici alle sedici."**

A che ora?	*At what time?*	**Alle otto.**	*At eight.*

The twenty-four hour clock is used for official timetables and it is safer to use it, to prevent any misunderstandings.

8,00	**alle otto**	8,45	**alle otto e quarantacinque**
8,15	**alle otto e quindici**	0,05	**a mezzanotte e cinque**
8,30	**alle otto e trenta**	1,50	**all'una e cinquanta**

Checkpoints

Can you . . . ?   **Yes**   **No**

- *ask if there is a good restaurant near here*. . . . . ❑ . . . . . . ❑
  C'è un buon ristorante qui vicino?

- *ask where a place is located* . . . . ❑ . . . . . . ❑
  Dov'è il museo nazionale?
  Dove si trova la farmacia?

- *understand directions* . . . . ❑ . . . . . . ❑
  La prima a destra, la terza a sinistra, dritto.

- *understand precise directions* . . . . ❑ . . . . . . ❑
  All'incrocio giri a destra.
  Davanti all'albergo.

- *ask if it's far* . . . . ❑ . . . . . . ❑
  È lontano?

- *understand how far it is* . . . . ❑ . . . . . . ❑
  È a cinquanta metri.

- *understand how long it will take* . . . . ❑ . . . . . . ❑
  È a cinque minuti.

- *say you've got the wrong road* . . . . ❑ . . . . . . ❑
  Ho sbagliato strada.

- *ask someone to repeat more slowly* . . . . ❑ . . . . . . ❑
  Può ripetere più lentamente?

- *understand commands* . . . . ❑ . . . . . . ❑
  Prenda!
  Giri!
  Torni indietro!

- *say what you and your friends are doing*. ❑ . . . . . . ❑
  Andiamo in centro.
  Prendiamo un caffè.

- *ask about opening and closing times* . . . . ❑ . . . . . . ❑
  A che ora apre la banca?
  A che ora chiudono i negozi?

- *understand the twenty-four hour clock* . . . . ❑ . . . . . . ❑
  Alle diciotto e venti.

- *say the days of the week* . . . . ❑ . . . . . . ❑
  Lunedì, martedì, mercoledì, giovedì, venerdì, sabato e domenica.

Learning tips

It is a good idea to record yourself repeating dialogues so that you can compare your efforts with the pronunciation of the Italian speakers.

Do you want to learn more?

Use the text as imaginatively as possible, for example, using the map on page 63 as a guide, you could draw a map of your own town center and give directions to an Italian tourist. Or you could write down the opening and closing times of shops, banks, and post offices in your own area.

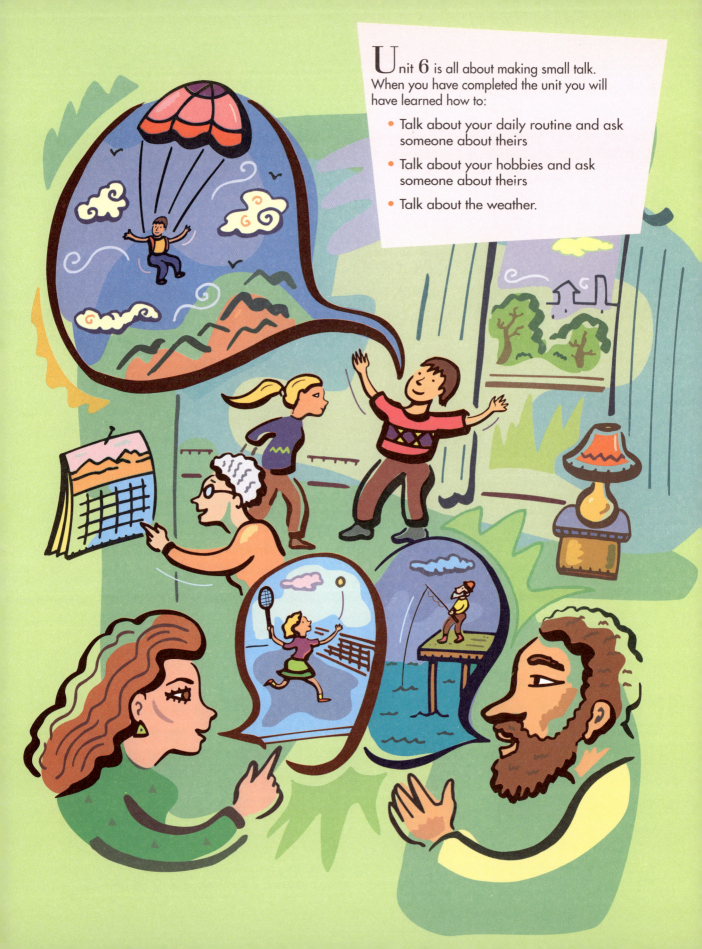

Unit 6 is all about making small talk. When you have completed the unit you will have learned how to:

- Talk about your daily routine and ask someone about theirs
- Talk about your hobbies and ask someone about theirs
- Talk about the weather.

La routine giornaliera 6

W o r d   B a n k

a casa	*at home*	fare colazione	*to have breakfast*
A che ora?	*At what time?*	fino a	*until*
a letto	*to bed*	guardare	*to watch*
alzarsi	*to get up*	il liceo classico	*classical high school*
ascoltare	*to listen to*	in macchina	*by car*
cenare	*to have supper*	il pranzo	*lunch*
comodo	*convenient*	rilassarsi	*to relax*
delle volte	*sometimes*	svegliarsi	*to wake up*
di solito	*usually*	il tempo	*time*
durante	*during*	tornare	*to return*
Esce?	*Do you go out? (formal)*	l'ufficio	*office*
		verso	*about*

A che ora si alza?

Talking about your daily routine

RECORDING

1. **Listen to Mr. Rossi answering some questions about his daily routine.**

A che ora si sveglia?	*At what time do you wake up?*
Fa colazione?	*Do you have breakfast?*
La domenica c'è più tempo.	*On Sundays, there is more time.*
Va al lavoro in macchina?	*Do you go to work by car?*
Arrivo in ufficio alle otto e un quarto.	*I arrive at the office at a quarter past eight.*
Torno a casa e mi rilasso.	*I return home and relax.*

2. **Listen to the dialog again and fill in the timetable of: a. signor Rossi's day; b. your own day; c. you and your partner's day**

	Si sveglia e si alza	Mi sveglio e mi alzo	Ci svegliamo e ci alziamo
7,00			
7,45			
8,15			
13,30			
15,00			
19,00			
20,00			

3. **You meet Mrs. Ragusa, a teacher, and her daughter Silvia and would like to find out about their daily routine. Supply the missing questions.**

Signora Ragusa   **Silvia**

1. A che ora si sveglia?   _____

2. _____   Quando fai colazione?

3. A che ora esce di casa?   _____

4. _____   Vai a scuola in macchina?

5. A che ora arriva a scuola?   _____

4.

Listen to the head teacher of a school talking about his typical day. Can you fill in the blanks?

Io _____ il preside di un liceo classico. La mattina _____ presto verso le sei. _____ un caffè e _____ lentamente. Non _____ colazione. _____ e _____ di casa alle otto meno venti e _____ a scuola a piedi perché è qui vicino. _____ il lavoro alle otto. C'è sempre molto da fare. _____ il lavoro all'una e mezzo e _____ a casa. Con mia moglie _____ il pranzo e _____ verso le due e mezzo. Il pomeriggio _____ un po'. _____ il giornale o un libro o _____ la televisione. Quando c'è una riunione _____ a scuola alle quattro. Altrimenti _____ al computer per un po'. Delle volte la sera _____ con gli amici o qualche volta _____ a teatro o ad un concerto.

Your turn

Now tell us something about yourself.

1. Che lavoro fa?
2. A che ora si alza la mattina?
3. Quando esce di casa?
4. Come va al lavoro?
5. A che ora torna a casa?
6. Che cosa fa la sera?

Close-up

The twelve-hour clock follows the same basic principle as the twenty-four hour clock, but you will need to know how to say the following:

24-hour Clock	12-hour Clock
at 12,00	a mezzogiorno
at 24,00	a mezzanotte
at 7,15	alle sette e un quarto
at 15,30	alle tre e mezzo
at 17,45	alle sei meno un quarto

Si sveglia, *from the infinitive* **svegliarsi,** *meaning "to wake up", and* **si alza** (**alzarsi,** *"to get up") follow the same pattern as* **chiamarsi.**

Che cosa Le piace fare il weekend?

Talking about weekend activities

Word Bank

andare a cavallo	*to go on horseback*	la neve	*snow*
l'autunno	*autumn*	nuotare	*swim*
cantare	*to sing*	qualche	*some*
il coro	*choir*	qualche volta	*sometime*
l'estate (f)	*summer*	la pallacanestro	*basketball*
frequentare	*to attend, frequent*	la primavera	*spring*
giocare	*to play*	sciare	*to ski*
l'inverno	*winter*	suonare	*to play (a musical instrument)*
leggere	*to read*		
il mare	*sea*	viaggiare	*to travel*
la montagna	*mountain*	la volta	*time, occasion*

1. **Marcello and Nadia are talking about what they like to do on weekends. Repeat the dialog.**

Il sabato sera vado al cinema.	*On Saturday evenings I go to the movies.*
Che cosa fate?	*What do you do?*
Se c'è neve, andiamo in montagna.	*If there's snow, we go to the mountains.*
Ci piace molto sciare.	*We like skiing a lot.*
D'estate andiamo al mare.	*In summer we go to the seashore.*

2. **Listen again and correct the following sentences:**

1. Marcello e Nadia vanno al cinema il venerdì sera.

2. D'inverno se non c'è neve vanno a sciare.

3. La domenica, d'inverno e d'estate nuotano e fanno windsurf.

3. *Listen to Maria talking about what she does at various times of the year and number the activities in the order in which you hear them.*

a. _____

b. _____

c. _____

d. _____

e. _____

f. _____

g. _____

h. _____

i. _____

4. *Listen to Maria talking about what she likes doing once again and enter each activity next to the appropriate season.*

d'estate	_____	_____	_____	_____
d'inverno	_____	_____	_____	_____
in primavera	_____	_____	_____	_____
in autunno	_____	_____	_____	_____

5. *Fill in the table for each of the activities that Maria likes to do. Follow the example given below.*

Io	Guido ed io	i miei amici
gioco a tennis	giochiamo a tennis	giocano a tennis

6. *Look at the activities listed and write down what you like to do and what you don't like to do using either* **mi piace** *or* **non mi piace.**

Example: Mi piace viaggiare.

viaggiare	leggere	giocare a carte
ballare	suonare il pianoforte	fare windsurf
tornare a casa la sera	alzarmi presto	mangiare

Your turn

You are talking to your Italian friend about your hobbies. Listen to the prompts on the recording and play your part.

Close-up

You have learned to use **mi piace**, "I like," in Unit 2. Notice that you can also use this expression with a verb to say "I like doing..."

Mi piace sciare.   *I like skiing. (literally "skiing is pleasing to me")*

Ci piace sciare.   *We like skiing. (**ci** = "to us")*

Ti piace viaggiare?   *Do you like to travel? (**ti** = "to you")*

When you use **mi piace** with a reflexive verb like **alzarsi**, you have to remember to change the final **si** as appropriate.

Non **mi** piace alzar**mi** presto.   *I don't like getting up early.*
        (literally "I don't like getting myself up")

Notice how **Qualche,** "some," is used in Italian:

Qualche volta. *Sometimes.*   **Qualche** amico. *Some friends.*

It is always used with a singular noun, not with the plural as in English.

We say **giocare**, meaning "to play", but "we play" is **giochiamo.** Why add the **h?** You have already seen that when **c** or **g** are followed by **e** or **i,** they become soft. For example, **c** is pronounced "ch" and **g** as "j". In verbs (such as **giocare**) where the "c" sound is hard, in order to keep the hard sound, add an **h** whenever the **c** is followed by **e** or **i.** Many verbs ending in **–care** or **–gare** follow this pattern.

Attività e passatempi

Talking about pastimes and the weather

Word Bank

l'allenamento	*training*	in luglio	*in July*
altro	*other*	la nebbia	*fog*
anche se	*even if*	nevicare	*to snow*
brutto/a	*ugly, bad*	ogni	*every*
il calcio	*soccer*	la palestra	*gymnasium*
caldo	*hot, warm*	la partita	*game*
correre	*to run*	piovere	*to rain*
discretamente	*quite well*	praticare	*practice*
la donna	*woman*	preferito	*favorite*
in effetti	*in fact*	la soddisfazione	*satisfaction*
freddo	*cold*	il sole	*sun*
giocare	*to play*	il torneo	*tournament*

1.   *Listen to Matteo talking about his sporting activities.*
Then repeat the conversation.

Tu giochi a pallacanestro?   *Do you play basketball?*

Quante volte alla settimana fai l'allenamento?   *How many times a week do you train?*

Ogni giorno corro.   *I run every day.*

Anche se piove?   *Even if it rains?*

Anche quando fa brutto tempo.   *Even if the weather's bad.*

Pratichi altri sport?   *Do you do other sports?*

2.   *Listen again to the conversation and answer the*
questions.

1. Qual è lo sport preferito di Matteo?

2. Quante volte alla settimana fa l'allenamento?

3. Che cosa fa ogni giorno?

4. Quando c'è la partita di pallacanestro?

5. Che cosa fa Matteo il sabato?

6. Che sport pratica d'estate?

7. Che tempo fa a luglio?

3.   *Read the weather conditions in Column 1 and find an*
appropriate action in Column 2.

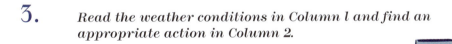

1. Se c'è neve   a. vado a sciare

2. Se fa caldo   b. non esco in macchina

3. Se c'è vento   c. vado al mare

4. Se fa freddo   d. vado al cinema

5. Se c'è nebbia   e. faccio windsurf

4.

Listen to the months of the year and repeat them.

i mesi

gennaio	febbraio	marzo	aprile
maggio	giugno	luglio	agosto
settembre	ottobre	novembre	dicembre

Trenta giorni ha novembre

con aprile, giugno e settembre

di ventotto ce n'è uno,

tutti gli altri ne hanno trentuno.

5.

You are thinking of going to Italy in March and are wondering where to go. Listen as an Italian friend gives you a summary of the weather forecast to help you make up your mind. Jot down the details below. The first one is already done for you.

Example: Sulle Alpi nevica e fa molto freddo.

Che tempo fa?

1. sulle Alpi   2. a Venezia   3. in Val Padana

4. a Roma   5. a Bari   6. a Palermo

6.

Keeping in mind what you have heard in the previous recordings, answer the following questions.

1. Che tempo fa nella Sua città in estate?

   _____.

2. Nel mese di gennaio dove fa più caldo, a Palermo o a Chicago?

   _____.

3. Perché non è una buon' idea andare a Venezia durante luglio
   e agosto? _____.

4. Qual è il mese dell'anno quando Lei va in cerca di sole?

   _____.

5. Nel nord d'Italia com'è il tempo in febbraio e in marzo?

   _____.

Your turn

*Now tell us a little more about yourself. Answer the
following questions.*

1. A che ora finisce il lavoro e che cosa fa dopo?

2. Quale sport preferisce?

3. Le piace praticare questo sport o solo guardare?

4. Quante volte all'anno va in vacanza e quando?

5. Dove va in vacanza?

6. Che cosa Le piace fare in vacanza?

7. Che tempo preferisce? Quando fa molto caldo, ad esempio, o
   quando fa freddo?

Did You Know?

Temperatures can vary considerably in Italy. It is generally accepted that
mid-summer is not the best time to visit Venice because of the humidity,
but be prepared for the possibility of chilly winds from the north if you go
in spring. It is, of course, always worth going in February for the Carnival
whatever the weather. But boots are essential as Saint Mark's Square is often
flooded. In winter, Val Padana, the Po Valley, is renowned for its thick fog,
so go further north to the beautiful ski resorts in the Dolomites and the Alps.
South of Rome, winters are very mild except on high ground, and summers
are hot.

Pronunciation

1. *If you listen carefully to the following double consonants, you should be able to hear that they sound longer than the single consonant. Repeat them as accurately as you can.*

nebbia   piuttosto   macchina

pallacanestro   autunno   freddo

Now listen to the following words and decide whether they have a single or a double consonant.

1. b? bb?	2. b? bb?	3. d? dd?
4. d? dd?	5. t? tt?	6. t? tt?
7. c? cc?	8. c? cc?	9. l? ll?
10. l? ll?	11. n? nn?	12. n? nn?

2. *Remember that the stress changes in the third person plural of verbs. The normal stress is on the penultimate syllable:* **com**prate, *but in the third person plural, it is on the prepenultimate, or next-to-last two syllables:* **com**prano. *Try saying the following examples:*

chiudete—chiudono   aprite—aprono

giocate—giocano   comprate—comprano

mangiate—mangiano   lavorate—lavorano

finite—finiscono

Close up

Notice how you say "to play football" to play tennis, and so forth:

giocare a calcio   **giocare a** tennis

To say "how often/how many times" use **quante volte.**

How many times...	a day?	Quante volte **al** giorno?
	a week?	Quante volte **alla** settimana?
	a month?	Quante volte **al** mese?
	a year?	Quante volte **all'**anno?

Notice again how **a, al, alla,** or **all'** is used in this construction.

When talking about the weather, we usually use the verb **fare.**

| Fa caldo. | It's hot. | Fa freddo. | It's cold. |
| Fa bello. | The weather's nice. | Fa brutto. | The weather's horrible. |

But:

Piove.	It's raining.	Nevica.	It's snowing.
C'è vento.	It's windy.	C'è nebbia.	It's foggy.
C'è sole.	It's sunny.		

Different prepositions are used to talk about where you are or where you are going depending on the type of place. If you are talking about a town, you use **a:**

Siamo **a** Venezia.

With the name of a region or country, you usually use **in:**

Siamo **in** Val Padana.   Andiamo **in** Italia.

There are also some set expressions:

In montagna.

Al mare.

Al cinema.

A teatro.

Sulle Alpi.

Checkpoints

Can you...?   **Yes**   **No**

- *say what you do every day* . . . . ☐ . . . . . . ☐
  Mi alzo alle sette.

- *ask what someone usually does* . . . . ☐ . . . . . . ☐
  Che cosa fa la sera?

- *ask what time someone does something* . . . . ☐ . . . . . . ☐
  A che ora?
  Quando?

- *say what you like doing* . . . . ☐ . . . . . . ☐
  Mi piace sciare.

- *ask what someone else likes doing* . . . . ☐ . . . . . . ☐
  Che cosa Le piace fare?
  Che cosa ti piace fare?

- *talk about your pastimes* . . . . ☐ . . . . . . ☐
  Gioco a calcio.
  Guardo la tivù.
  Faccio l'allenamento.

- *Talk about the weather* . . . . ☐ . . . . . . ☐
  Fa caldo.
  C'è sole.
  Piove.

- *say what you do if...* . . . . ☐ . . . . . . ☐
  Se c'è vento faccio windsurf.

- *ask how many times* . . . . ☐ . . . . . . ☐
  Quante volte alla settimana?

- *say sometimes, usually* . . . . ☐ . . . . . . ☐
  Qualche volta, delle volte, di solito

- *talk about what people do in different seasons, months* . . . . ☐ . . . . . . ☐
  Giochiamo a tennis d'estate.
  Vado a cavallo in primavera.
  Viaggia d'autunno.
  Sciamo in gennaio.
  Nuoto in (a) luglio.

Learning tips

It is helpful to learn the patterns of regular verbs ending in **-are, -ere,** *and* **-ire** *so that you can recognize them easily and quickly. Since Italians generally do not use the words for the pronouns "I", "you", "he", "she", and "it", you will need to recognize the forms of the verb in order to understand who they are talking about.*

Do you want to learn more?

Since this unit deals with routines and hobbies, make a point of telling yourself what you are doing in Italian throughout the day. This will help you to remember the words you have learned in the unit.

1 _Extra_!

1. _Greet these people and ask them how they are. Notice the time of day. How do you think each one would reply?_

Example: Buongiorno, signor Pasini. Come sta?

Sto benissimo, grazie. E Lei?

RECORDING

2. _Read and listen to this travel ad._

Immagina un po'! Dove sei? No, no, no, non sei più qui. Entri in un sogno. Guarda bene la foto! Sei su una spiaggia deserta. Il mare è calmo, limpido e caldo. Prova un po'! È caldo, vero? Questa sensazione è deliziosa e molto rilassante. È un vero paradiso. La Sicilia ti aspetta. L'Italia ti aspetta...

3. *Listen to Activity 2 again and match the two columns!*

1. Perché non sei qui?
2. Dove sei?
3. Il mare è agitato, sporco e freddo?
4. Questa è una sensazione orribile?
5. È stressante?
6. Dov'è questo paradiso personale?

a. Sono su una spiaggia deserta.
b. No, è molto rilassante.
c. È in Sicilia.
d. Perché entro in un sogno.
e. No, è calmo, limpido e caldo.
f. No, è deliziosa.

4. *This is the letter that David Sutton sent to the Mayor of Scillato in an attempt to trace his long lost Italian aunt. Complete the letter with the missing words. You will have to consult the glossary to understand it all. The key below to the asterisked words will tell you what to look for.*

italiana	cognome	chiamo	è
abita	sono	dove	questo

Gentile Sindaco,

Mi _____ David Sutton e _____ americano. Mia madre è di origine italiana e io cerco* una mia zia _____. Non so* se mia zia _____ ancora viva. Il suo _____ è Catalisano. Non so* neanche _____ abita ma forse _____ a Scillato. Mia madre ricorda* _____ nome.

Le sarei* molto grato per il Suo aiuto nel trovare mia zia.

Distinti saluti

David Sutton

*cerco — cercare   *so — sapere   *ricorda — ricordare
* sarei = *I would be*

2 *Extra!*

Faccio l'insegnante

1. *Look at the columns below, one contains a list of occupations and the other a list of what each person does. Try matching the two!*

1. un cuoco   a. ripara
2. un autista   b. cucina
3. un meccanico   c. cura
4. un medico   d. guida
5. un insegnante   e. suona
6. un musicista   f. insegna

2. *Have you seen the film,* Il postino? *It is an enchanting love story set on one of Italy's beautiful islands. Listen to the short summary of the film and answer the questions below in Italian.*

1. Che tipo di film è *Il postino*?
2. Mario lavora all'inizio del film?
3. Chi è Beatrice?
4. Chi è Neruda?
5. Perché ha bisogno di un postino?
6. Di chi è innamorato Mario?
7. Perché trova difficoltà in questa situazione?
8. Con l'aiuto del poeta Neruda, che cosa fa Mario?

3.

Italians are renowned for their spirit of enterprise and Italy is a country with many cars and very few parking lots. In the southern part of the country, where there is a great deal of unemployment, some people manage to find work in a creative ways. Read the job description below and answer the questions in English.

Disoccupazione e fantasia.

Il custode di parcheggio abusivo.

Chi è?
È un disoccupato con molta fantasia.

Dove lavora?
Lavora normalmente in una grande piazza o in strada dove normalmente c'è posto per parcheggiare.

Che cosa fa?
Aiuta l'automobilista a trovare un posteggio e sorveglia le macchine. Se non c'è un posteggio, l'automobilista lascia la chiave della macchina al custode. L'automobilista paga per questo servizio.

Perché è abusivo?
Perché il custode fa questo lavoro per conto suo e non è autorizzato.

1. *What kind of person is this parking attendant?*

2. *Where does he work?*

3. *What does he do?*

4. *What if no space is immediately available?*

5. *Why is this work considered illegal?*

4.

*If you are a qualified teacher in Italy, you do not apply for a teaching post that becomes vacant. Instead there is a system of **concorsi**. This system applies for all public servants. Read on! Then answer the questions in English.*

Un concorso è una prova di selezione con esami per assumere impiegati statali. Scenario: Studio francese all'università per diventare insegnante ma non è tanto facile. C'è un concorso ma solo ogni quattro anni perché in questo momento non c'è bisogno di insegnanti. Se sono promosso al concorso, non decido io dove insegno. È il Ministero della Pubblica Istruzione che decide dove c'è bisogno di insegnanti e sono nominato ad un posto anche lontano da dove abito.

1. *What is a **concorso**?*

2. *If I wish to become a teacher, how often is there a* **concorso**?

3. *Can you explain why?*

4. *If I pass, who decides where I will teach and on what basis?*

3 *Extra!*

La famiglia e gli amici

1. *Who am I? Identify the family members.*

1. Se io sono il fratello della tua mamma?

2. Se io sono il padre di tua moglie?

3. Se io sono la sorella di tuo marito?

4. Se io sono il figlio della sorella di tuo padre?

5. Se io sono il marito di tua figlia?

6. Se io sono il fratello di tua figlia?

RECORDING

2. *Elisabetta Ferracini, a popular Italian TV hostess talks about her mother, Mara Venier. Listen and answer the questions.*

1. Dove lavora Elisabetta?

2. Dove lavora la sua mamma?

3. Che cos'è Solletico?

4. Com'è Mara secondo Elisabetta?

5. Com'è una tipica mamma italiana?

6. Che cosa fa Mara quando perde la pazienza?

N o t i z i e
Elisabetta Ferracini: «Mara Venier, la mia brava mamma italiana»

Come mamma lavora in tivù: di pomeriggio, su Raiuno, conduce *Solletico*, programma per bambini. Ma, come mamma, piace anche ai grandi: quando appare con le sue minigonne colorate più di un papà si ferma a guardarla. Si chiama Elisabetta Ferracini, è conosciuta come la figlia di Mara Venier. Mamma ha sempre cercato di allontanarla dal mondo dello spettacolo, "però, come i figli degli avvocati si iscrivono alla facoltà di legge, io sono rimasta folgorata dalla televisione", dice Elisabetta. Ma è proprio in tutto uguale a mamma? "No, lei è golosa, io per nulla. Lei divora il cioccolato fondente. Io non mangio una fetta di salame da cinque anni. Vivo a riso bollito e verdure: credo di essere allergica a quasi tutti i cibi. Mara dice che sono manie. È la classica mamma italiana, protettiva e severa. E quando perde la pazienza urla come una pazza. Però non porta rancore".

3. *Read the small ads below and decide which one you*
would choose in each of the following cases.

1. *If you were a single man of about 40, looking for someone*
   sociable and dynamic with a love of life, but also with a
   romantic side to their personality?

2. *If you were a serious man aged between 45 and 50 and you*
   were looking for someone attractive and economically
   independent?

3. *If you were a 33-year-old woman with a good job who liked*
   sports and the seashore?

4. *If you were a 50-year-old single woman?*

38enne professionista, laureato, sportivo, amante del mare, cerca donna max. 35enne, buona posizione socio-economica per costruire futuro insieme.

a.

Divorziato giovanile 47 anni cerca brava donna, vedova, signorina, separata, divorziata, anche straniera per rapporto di amicizia, eventuale matrimonio.

b.

Ho 35 anni, sono impiegata, sono di carattere socievole, allegra, dinamica, amo la vita. Spero di incontrare la mia anima gemella.

c.

Donna 35enne, bella presenza, alta, economicamente indipendente, cerca uomo max. 50enne, serio, socievole, allegro per amicizia, eventuale matrimonio.

d.

4. *Could you help me write a personal ad for an Italian*
newspaper?

I am a 30-year-old divorced woman with one child. I am
economically independent, good-looking, and sociable. I am
looking for a man not more than 40 years of age. He should be
dynamic, enjoy sports, and love the seashore.

4 *Extra* !

Qualcosa da mangiare o da bere?

1. *Stereotypes should help you unscramble the jumbled words in this activity.*

1. I tedeschi bevono - - - - -   RIBAR
2. Gli italiani bevono - - - - -   FEFAC
3. I francesi bevono - - - - - - - - -   ORIVSOSON
4. Gli inglesi bevono - - - - - - - - -   ATLETELTA
5. Gli americani bevono - - - - - - - -   AOCALOCC

2. *Listen to the recording and decide whether the waiter has got the order correct. If not, what mistakes has he made?*

3. *Read the advertisement for this road atlas and answer the questions!*

1. *List the important selling features of this road atlas.*

2. *How up-to-date is it?*

3. *What present is given with it?*

4. *Listen to this publicity spot and answer the questions below!*

1. *How many volumes are there in this series on Britain?*

2. *What are the other titles in the series in English?*

3. *What chapters does this guidebook consist of?*

4. *What is contained in the introduction?*

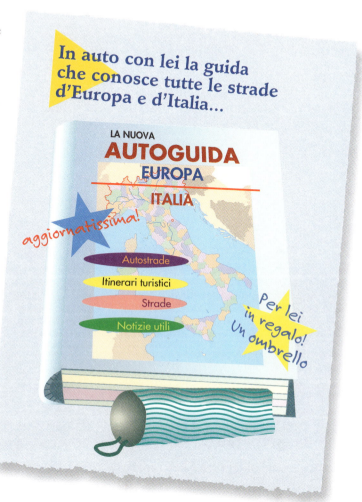

In auto con lei la guida che conosce tutte le strade d'Europa e d'Italia...

LA NUOVA
AUTOGUIDA
EUROPA
ITALIA

aggiornatissima!

Autostrade
Itinerari turistici
Strade
Notizie utili

Per lei in regalo! Un ombrello

RECORDING

1. *You are on a guided tour of Rome. Listen carefully to your Italian guide. First, check (✓) the sites you hear mentioned from the list below, then number the sites mentioned in the order in which you hear them on the recording.*

_____ il Colosseo   _____ Piazza Navona

_____ il Foro Romano   _____ la fontana di Trevi

_____ la chiesa di Santa Maria Maggiore   _____ il museo nazionale

_____ Piazza Venezia   _____ Piazza di Spagna

_____ il Pantheon   _____ Via del Corso

_____ la Galleria di arte antica

2.   *Read the following excerpts from a guidebook to Rome
and answer the questions!*

ROMA E FEDE

Da vedere! Due statue e due tombe!

Nella Basilica di San Pietro a destra, c'è l'incomparabile statua in marmo bianco della Pietà di Michelangelo che merita almeno cinque minuti di contemplazione.

A sinistra a venti metri circa, c'è il Tesoro di San Pietro. Qui c'è una vera sorpresa - una seconda Pietà questa volta in gesso. È la prova per la statua in marmo.

Gli Scavi

Nella cripta, c'è la splendida cappella dorata di San Pietro. Ma per vedere la vera tomba di San Pietro in tutta la sua semplicità, visitate gli scavi sotto la Basilica. L'Ufficio degli Scavi si trova nel Vaticano. L'entrata è a sinistra della cattedrale sotto l'arco dove c'è la guardia svizzera.

1. *Where would you find the first famous statue by Michelangelo?*

2. *And where would you find the second?*

3. *What is the difference between the two?*

4. *Why are there two?*

5. *Where would you find the official tomb of Saint Peter and what does it look like?*

6. *Where would you find the actual tomb and how does it differ?*

7. *Where is the Excavations Office?*

8. *How do you get to it?*

9. *Who will you have to pass?*

6 Extra!

La routine giornaliera

RECORDING

1. *Listen to Mr. Vinci being interviewed about his daily routine and fill in the blanks in the passage below with the appropriate form of the verb.*

Il signor Vinci _____ (essere) tipografo. _____ (lavorare) per il giornale di Sicilia.

_____ (fare) il turno di notte. Il lavoro _____ (cominciare) a mezzanotte e _____ (finire) alle sei di mattina. Quando _____ (arrivare) a casa, non _____ (andare) subito a letto. _____ (fare) colazione con la famiglia e poi _____ (riposarsi) un po'.

Alle dieci _____ (uscire) con la moglie o _____ (incontrare) gli amici. Non _____ (sentirsi) stanco perché _____ (essere) abituato a questo ritmo di vita. I suoi figli _____ (tornare) a casa all'una e mezzo e _____ (pranzare) tutti insieme. Verso le due e mezzo _____ (andare) a letto e _____ (cominciare) la sua 'notte'. Lui _____ (alzarsi) verso le nove di sera e _____ (cenare) con la famiglia. Dopo cena _____ (guardare) la tivù o _____ (ascoltare) la musica. _____ (uscire) di casa alle undici e mezzo. Durante la notte _____ (fare) uno spuntino e _____ (bere) molti caffè.

2. *The passage on pages A13 to A14 is adapted from a guidebook to Italy. It tells you the best time to visit certain areas. Imagine that you are going to visit Milan, Venice, Florence, Rome, and the islands of Sicily and Sardinia. First find them on the map, then write short notes on the climate, the best time to visit and times to avoid.*

Quando partire per l'Italia - una guida per il turista.

Italia - Paese del sole? Se è vero per la Riviera e per il Sud, non è altrettanto vero per il resto del paese.

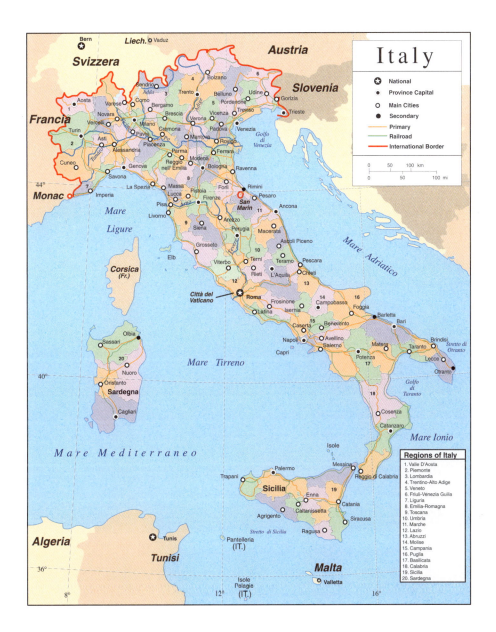

Italy

- ✪ National
- ● Province Capital
- ○ Main Cities
- ● Secondary
- ── Primary
- ── Railroad
- ── International Border

| 0 | 50 | 100 km |
| 0 | 50 | 100 mi |

Regions of Italy
1. Valle D'Aosta
2. Piemonte
3. Lombardia
4. Trentino-Alto Adige
5. Veneto
6. Friuli-Venezia Giulia
7. Liguria
8. Emilia-Romagna
9. Toscana
10. Umbria
11. Marche
12. Lazio
13. Abruzzi
14. Molise
15. Campania
16. Puglia
17. Basilicata
18. Calabria
19. Sicilia
20. Sardegna

● Nel nord dell'Italia, c'è una differenza fra il clima montano delle Alpi e delle Dolomiti (dove ci sono numerose località di sport invernali e dunque molta neve, ma anche molto sole) e il clima mite della regione dei laghi (Maggiore, Como, Garda) e del litorale ligure, da Ventimiglia a Livorno, dove l'inverno è dolce, secco e luminoso, e l'estate calda con molto sole.

- La Val Padana ha inverni freddi e nuvolosi; le temperature a Milano sono basse e spesso c'è nebbia. D'estate c'è sole ma è una stagione calda e afosa con frequenti temporali.

- Sul mare Adriatico a Rimini ad esempio, fa un caldo più sopportabile d'estate ed è un posto molto frequentato dai turisti in cerca di sole. D' inverno, su questo litorale, c'è un vento freddo che si chiama la bora. Venezia è da evitare a luglio e soprattutto ad agosto quando c'è molta umidità e ci sono troppi turisti. Ma è da visitare per il Carnevale a febbraio anche se non fa molto bello.

- A Firenze e nelle regioni dell'Italia centrale, il clima invernale è abbastanza piovoso ma piuttosto mite, eccetto sugli Appennini, dove c'è spesso vento. Da maggio a settembre, il tempo caldo, assolato, asciutto consente un soggiorno piacevole in Toscana. Ad ottobre c'è più pioggia e a novembre e dicembre il cielo è spesso molto nuvoloso.

- In tutto il sud, a partire da Roma, l'estate è caldissima, secca e assolata sul litorale e a volte torrida sulle colline e nelle pianure interne, in particolare in Sardegna e in Sicilia, soprattutto quando soffia lo scirocco, vento secco e molto caldo proveniente dall'Africa. Delle volte, d'estate, ci sono violenti temporali. D'inverno il clima è molto mite ma la primavera è un buon periodo per visitare il sud dell'Italia, la Sicilia e la Sardegna, soprattutto nei mesi di maggio e di giugno; a Pasqua il bel tempo non è sempre garantito. Roma è da visitare in ogni momento dell'anno.

Test 1:

Review of Units 1–3

1. *Write out the missing numbers in each problem.*

1. undici   +   _____   = quindici

2. cinque   +   _____   = otto

3. dieci   +   _____   = diciannove

4. venti   –   _____   = tre

5. tredici   –   _____   = due

6. diciannove –   _____   = cinque

2. *Which word or expression does not belong in each group?*

1. figlia	amico	cugino	fratello	nonno
2. ingegnere	meccanico	maschio	insegnante	parrucchiere
3. arrivederci	ciao	arrivederLa	a presto	sto bene
4. abbastanza bene	male	non c'è male	mi chiamo	benissimo
5. tre	quattordici	quanto	nove	diciassette
6. tempo	giorno	mese	anno	settimana

3. *Complete the sentences with the appropriate form of the definite article* **il, lo, l', la, i, gli,** *or* **le**.

1. _____ signora Bini non parla tedesco, ma _____ signor Bini parla francese.

2. Non ho _____ orologio, ma sono _____ dieci e mezzo.

3. _____ amici e _____ amiche di Laura sono simpatici.

4. _____ zio di Rita è allo stadio con _____ nonni.

5. _____ figlio e _____ figlia di Giacomo sono gemelli.

6. _____ amica di Laura è bionda e _____ ragazzo è bruno.

4. *Choose the appropriate response.*

1. Di dove sei? _____
(**Sono il signor Marini. / Sono di Milano. / Sto bene, grazie.**)

2. Ciao, Samanta! Come stai? _____
(**Sono a casa. / Sto benissimo. / Sono infermiera.**)

3. Quanti anni hai? _____
(**Trenta. / Ho un fratello. / Da dieci anni.**)

4. È sposato? _____
(**Sì, è spagnolo. / No, è avvocato. / No, è divorziato.**)

5. Che lavoro fa? _____
(**No, ho uno studio. / Faccio il medico. / Due minuti fa.**)

6. Per quanto tempo sta qui? _____
(**Da un anno. / Per trovare un lavoro. / Per tre mesi.**)

5. *From these jumbled letters find the names of six jobs or occupations .*

1. rucrarpachie   4. ferrainmie

2. geinregne   5. tovocava

3. gnasetenin   6. cimode

6. *Answer each question negatively and give the correct information.*

Example: Mara è americana? No, è italiana.

1. I Beatles sono giapponesi?

2. Luciano Pavarotti è tedesco?

3. Sofia Loren è inglese?

4. Barbara Walters è russa?

5. Al Pacino è francese?

6. Brigitte Bardot e Catherine Deneuve sono italiane?

7. *Circle the correct word.*

1. **Sua/La sua** famiglia è grande.

2. **Mio/Il mio** fratello ha sedici anni.

3. Luciano vive con **sua/la sua** ragazza.

4. Ecco **tuo/il tuo** marito.

5. Oggi vedo **mia/la mia** mamma.

6. Cosa fa **tua/la tua** figlia?

8. *Write two questions (formal and informal) for each of the following answers.*

Example: Mi chiamo Mara Martini.   Come si chiama? Come ti chiami?

1. Sono di Firenze.   4. Ho una figlia.

2. Ho trentacinque anni.   5. Faccio l'insegnante.

3. Sì, sono sposata.

9. *Choose the words from the right column to form a logical sentence with the words from the left column.*

1. Mio marito ha 37 anni   a. da due mesi.

2. Faccio   b. questa città?

3. Mio figlio   c. la ragioniera.

4. Le piace   d. bella e simpatica.

5. Abito qui   e. ma io ho 33 anni.

6. Mia sorella è   f. lavora per la Fiat.

10. *Underline each* **c** *that has a hard sound "k."*

Example: <u>ch</u>iamo
1. dieci   4. città   7. maschio   10. celibe

2. che   5. perché   8. piace

3. chi   6. suocera   9. ciao

Test 2:

1. *Which word or expression does not belong in each group?*

1. lunedì	mercoledì	venerdì	domenica	mattina
2. panino	pizzetta	cornetto	insalata	ciambella
3. giugno	autunno	gennaio	ottobre	aprile
4. fragola	vino	birra	tè	aranciata
5. via	posta	viale	corso	strada
6. di fronte	accanto	dietro	invece	in fondo

2. *Write the following times.*

Example: 9,00 Sono le nove.

1. 1,15   4. 17,45

2. 10,30   5. 20,50

3. 12,00   6. 24,00

3. *You are at a café in Rome. Call the waiter and order each of the following items using the indefinite article (* **un, uno una,** *or* **un'***).*

Example: cappuccino   Cameriere, un cappuccino!

1. caffè   4. birra

2. aranciata   5. scotch

3. Martini®   6. Coca-Cola®

4. *Choose the words from the right column to form a logical sentence with the words from the left column.*

1. D'estate	a. prendere un aperitivo.
2. La fermata dell'autobus	b. qui vicino?
3. Chiudono	c. fa caldo qui.
4. C'è un ristorante	d. alle 6,00.
5. Vorrei	e. da bere?
6. Che cosa vuoi	f. è davanti alla farmacia.

5. *Complete the sentences with the appropriate forms of* **a** *or* **in** *and the definite article as needed.*

1. Quest'estate vado _____ Francia.

2. Oggi resto _____ casa.

3. Mario va in vacanza _____ Stati Uniti.

4. Arriviamo _____ stazione di Firenze.

5. Se nevica Luisa va _____ montagna.

6. Mi piace molto andare _____ teatro.

7. L'avvocato arriva _____ ufficio _____ otto e mezzo.

6. *Write the correct form of the verb in parentheses.*

1. Signora, che cosa _____ (**prendere**)?

2. Io _____ (**preferire**) un gelato al limone.

3. Quanto _____ (**costare**) questo poster?

4. D'inverno noi _____ (**andare**) al cinema la domenica.

5. Marisa, a che ora _____ (**svegliarsi**) la mattina?

6. Mia moglie ed io non _____ (**litigare**) mai.

7. *Write the questions to the following answers.*

1. Prendiamo un panino al prosciutto.

2. Costano 5 euro l'uno.

3. Marco si alza alle 6,30.

4. A luglio fa caldo.

5. Samanta è mia figlia.

6. Il ristorante è davanti alla galleria d'arte.

8. *Circle the correct word.*

1. **Quando/Quanto** va a sciare?

2. **Dove/Dov'è** il duomo?

3. Domani **c'è/ci sono** la partita di calcio.

4. Quanto **costa/costano** queste cartoline?

5. **Ce n'è/ne** uno a cinquanta metri.

6. Il signor Mattei **ti svegli/si sveglia** molto presto.

9. *Choose the appropriate answer.*

1. Desidera? _____
   (**Prego!/ Vorrei un panino./ Offro io.**)

2. Con ghiaccio? _____
   (**No, grazie, senza./ No, grazie, non ho fame./ Basta così.**)

3. Fa bello oggi? _____
   (**Sì, fa freddo e c'è vento./ Sì, è brutto tempo./ Sì, c'è sole e fa caldo.**)

4. Come va in centro? _____
   (**In macchina./ Al cinema./ In montagna.**)

5. Quanto costa? _____
   (**Costano 7 euro./ Costa 2 euro./ A mezzanotte.**)

10. *Write down the month for each of the following holidays.*

1. *Mother's Day*   5. *Independence Day*

2. *Labor Day*   6. *St. Valentine's Day*

3. *Thanksgiving*   7. *Halloween*

4. *New Year's Day*

Answer Key

Unit 1

Pages 4–5

2. 1. *false*; 2. *true*; 3. *false*

5. 1. Brigitte Verdier è francese; 2. Gianni Guerzoni è italiano; 3. Ernst Giese è tedesco; 4. Noriko Tosheiba è giapponese; 5. Maria de Santez è spagnola; 6. Ludmila Gogoleff è russa

6. 1. Parla inglese?; 2. Parla russo?; 3. Parla spagnolo?; 4. Parla tedesco?; 5. Parla francese?; 6. Parla giapponese?

Pages 8–10

2. *Answers will vary.*

3. 1b; 2c; 3d; 4a

5. 1b; 2c; 3a

6. 3, 2, 1, 4

7. 1. Mi chiamo Brigitte. Sono francese di Parigi e parlo russo ma non molto bene. 2. Mi chiamo Ernst. Sono tedesco di Hannover e parlo inglese abbastanza bene. 3. Mi chiamo Noriko. Sono giapponese di Tokyo e parlo italiano ma solo un po'. 4. Mi chiamo Maria. Sono spagnola di Madrid e parlo tedesco abbastanza bene. 5. Mi chiamo Ludmila. Sono russa di Mosca e parlo spagnolo ma non molto bene.

Pages 11–12

2. 1c; 2a; 3b

3. 1. Come si chiama? / Come ti chiami?; 2. Di dov'è? / Sei di qui?; 3. Dove abita? / Dove abiti?; 4. Parla inglese? / Parli inglese?

5. a1; b4; c3; d2

Unit 2

Pages 18–20

2. 1d; 2a; 3b; 4c

4. 1.No, da due anni. 2. No, da tre settimane. 3. No, da quattro giorni. 4. No, da cinque giorni.

5. 1. il meccanico; 3. il medico; 4. l'infermiera; 5. l'insegnante; 6. lo studente; 7. la parrucchiera

6. il meccanico; l'impiegato; il medico; l'infermiera; l'insegnante; lo studente; la parrucchiera; l'idraulico; la ragioniera

Your turn: cognome: Biondi; nome: Marisa; lavoro: ragioniera; ditta: la Miele

Pages 23–25

2. 1b; 2b; 3a

4. 1b; 2e; 3a; 4c; 5d

Your turn: Da quanto tempo studi italiano? / Parla molto bene. / No, solo da tre mesi. / Per quanto tempo stai qui?

5. *Paul:* studente / 3 anni / imparare italiano / un mese; *Fabrizio:* ragioniere / 12 anni / lavoro / cinque giorni; *Anna Maria:* insegnante / 22 anni / vacanza / due settimane

6. 1b; 2d; 3c; 4a

Pages 27–28

2. 1d; 2a; 3b; 4c; 5e

3. a1; b5; c4; d2; e3

4. 1. Sì, mi piace molto. È simpatico. 2. Sì, mi piace molto. È interessante. 3. Sì, mi piace molto. È molto bella.

5. *Sample answers:* Come si chiama? Mi chiamo Ugo Fabrizzi. / Che lavoro fa? Faccio il medico. / Dove lavora? Lavoro in uno studio medico in Corso Rosselli.

Unit 3

Pages 34–36

2. 1. è divorziato; 2. non è vedovo; 3. ha due figli

4. 1. ventotto; 2. ventitrè; 3. ventinove; 4. trenta; 5. ventiquattro; 6. ventidue; 7. ventuno; 8. ventisei

5. Claudia: mia nonna; Gaetano: mio nonno; Luigi; mio padre; Domenica: mia madre; Giorgio: mio zio; Lucia: mia zia; Giovanni: mio fratello; Mariangela: mia sorella; Paola: mia cugina

6. Giorgio è suo zio; Paola è sua cugina; Lucia è sua zia; Mariangela è sua sorella

7. I. Domenica ha un fratello, Giorgio; 2. Francesca ha una sorella, Mariangela. 3. Gaetano e Claudia hanno quattro nipoti: Giovanni, Francesca, Mariangela e Paola.

Pages 38–39

2. I. separato / partner / figli; 2. ex-moglie / marito / figlio; 3.unico / genitori / divorziati / nuova

3. È separato. / Ha una nuova partner. / La sua ex-moglie ha un nuovo marito. / Lei ha una nuova famiglia.

4. I. i genitori; 2. i fratelli; 3. i fratelli; 4. le sorelle; 5. i figli; 6. i nipoti; 7. gli zii; 8. i cugini.

Your turn: Hai fratelli? / Come si chiama tuo fratello? / È più grande? / E tua sorella?

5. tuo padre; il tuo medico; la tua ragioniera; i tuoi genitori; tua cugina; la tua ex-moglie; le tue sorelle

Pages 41–42

2. I. indaffarato, stanco; 2. bella, alta, intelligente, affettuosa, simpatica; 3. sportivi, studiosi

3. I. Il marito di Marisa è molto indaffarato e spesso è stanco. 2. La ragazza di Matteo è bella, alta, intelligente e affettuosa. 3. I suoi amici sono sportivi e abbastanza studiosi.

4. I. Laura e suo marito sono contenti ed affettuosi. 2. Rossella è molto impegnata. 3. Pino è molto stanco. 4. Franco è bello e sportivo.

Your turn: Answers will vary.

Unit 4

Pages 48–50

2. birra 2; coca-cola 2; caffè 2; aranciata 3; vino bianco I; pizzetta I; tè 2; cappuccino I; paste 2; gelati 2

3. I. due birre; 2. una coca-cola; 3. due aranciate; 4. un caffè; 5. due gelati; 6. una spremuta; 7. due ciambelle; 8. un panino

4. *If you are a man:* Desidera?; E Lei, signore? E per Lei, signore? *If you are a woman:* Desidera? Prego, signora? Che cosa prende, signorina? E Lei, signora?

6. a5; b3; c1; d2; e4

Pages 53–54

2. un amaro senza ghiaccio; un succo di frutta (pera); un bicchiere di vino bianco

3. Offro io! Che cosa prendete?; Che cosa prendi, Antonietta?; E per te, Paolo?

5. I. *one, friend;* 2. *more than one, friend/acquaintance;* 3. *one, acquaintance;* 4. *one, friend;* 5. *more than one, friend/acquaintance*

Pages 56–57

2. I. *true;* 2. *false;* 3. *false;* 4. *false;* 5. *true*

3. a3; b1; c4; d2

4. I. Quanto costa la guida? 2. Quanto costano i poster? 3. Quanto costano i francobolli? 4. Quanto costa la piantina?

Unit 5

Pages 61–64

2. I. La seconda a destra. 2. La prima a sinistra. 3. La quarta a sinistra. 4. La terza a destra. 5. Sulla destra. 6. Sulla sinistra.

3. I. farmacia; 2. supermercato; 3. banca; 4. cabina telefonica; 5. buca delle lettere

4. I. *the National Museum;* 2. *the Colosseum;* 3. *the bar;* 4. *the Hotel Paradiso;* 5. *the Gallery of Modern Art*

5. I. Dov'è il duomo? 2. Dov'è il museo? 3. C'è una farmacia qui vicino? 4. Dov'è la galleria d'arte? 5. C'è un bar qui vicino? 6. C'è un cinema qui vicino?

6. 5, 2, I, 3, 6, 4

Pages 66–67

2. I. Ho sbagliato strada. 2. Ho sbagliato piazza. 4. Ho sbagliato città. 5. Ho sbagliato numero. 5. Ho sbagliato hotel.

3. I. *Take the second on the right.* 2. *Turn right.* 3. *Straight ahead.* 4. *Find the right answer.* 5. *Listen to the dialog.* 6. *Write.*

5. *Sample answers:* I. Il museo è accanto all'hotel. 2. La fermata è davanti all'hotel. 3. La galleria d'arte è dietro il museo. 4. La posta è in fondo. 5. I negozi principali sono di fronte alla posta.

6. alla stazione; al Colosseo; al Foro Romano; alla Basilica di San Pietro; all'ufficio; alla tomba

7. I. preferiamo; 2. prendiamo; 3. arriviamo; 4. visitiamo

2. 1. Perché chiude alle quattro e non c'è abbastanza tempo per vedere tutto. 2. Sì, sono tutti chiusi il pomeriggio. 3. I negozi aprono alle nove di mattina. 4. Chiudono alle diciannove e trenta. 5. I grandi negozi sì, i piccoli negozi, no: chiudono dall'una alle quattro.

3. il museo apre alle 09,30, chiude alle 14,00; la galleria apre alle 10,00, chiude alle 18,30; i negozi aperto dalle 09,00 alle 13,30 la mattina e dalle 16,00 alle 19,30 la sera; la banca è aperta dalle 08,30 alle 13,30 la mattina e dalle 15,00 alle 16,00 la sera.

5. *Answers will vary.*

Unit 6

Pages 76–77

2. 7,00: si sveglia e si alza / mi sveglio e mi alzo / ci svegliamo e ci alziamo; 7,45: esce di casa/esco di casa / usciamo di casa; 8,15: arriva in ufficio / arrivo in ufficio / arriviamo in ufficio; 13,30: va a pranzo / vado a pranzo / andiamo a pranzo; 15,00–19,00: lavora / lavoro / lavoriamo; 19,00: torna a casa e si rilassa / torno a casa e mi rilasso / torniamo a casa e ci rilassiamo; 20,00: cena / ceno / ceniamo

3. 1. (Silvia) A che ora ti svegli? 2. (Signora Ragusa) Quando fa colazione? 3. (Silvia) A che ora esci di casa? 4. (Signora Ragusa) Va a scuola in macchina? 5. (Silvia) A che ora arrivi a scuola?

4. faccio; mi alzo; Prendo; mi sveglio; faccio; Mi preparo; esco; vado; Comincio; Finisco; torno; preparo; pranziamo; ci riposiamo; Leggo; guardo; torno; lavoro; usciamo; andiamo

Your turn: Answers will vary.

Pages 78–80

2. 1. Marcello e Nadia vanno al cinema il sabato sera. 2. D'inverno se c'è neve vanno a sciare. 3. La domenica d'estate nuotano e fanno windsurf.

3. a2; b4; c5; d7; e9; f8; g1; h3; i6

4. d'estate: nuota, fa surf, va in discoteca; d'inverno: va a sciare, va al cinema o a teatro, guarda la televisione; in primavera: gioca a tennis, va a cavallo; in autunno: gioca a pallacanestro, ascolta la musica

5. Io: gioco a tennis, vado a cavallo, nuoto, faccio surf, vado in discoteca, ascolto la musica, vado a sciare, vado al cinema o a teatro, guardo la televisione.

Guido ed io: giochiamo a tennis, andiamo a cavallo, nuotiamo, facciamo surf, andiamo in discoteca, ascoltiamo la musica, andiamo a sciare, andiamo al cinema o a teatro, guardiamo la televisione.

I miei amici: giocano a tennis, vanno a cavallo, nuotano, fanno surf, vanno in discoteca, ascoltano la musica, vanno a sciare, vanno al cinema o a teatro, guardano la televisione.

6. *Answers will vary.*

Your turn: Torno a casa alle sei e mezzo. / Ceno verso le sette e mezzo e di solito guardo la tivù o ascolto la musica. / Sì, esco con gli amici. / Andiamo al cinema o a teatro. / Non molto, ma d'estate nuoto e gioco a tennis.

Pages 83–85

2. 1. La pallacanestro. 2. Fa allenamento due volte alla settimana, il lunedì e il giovedì. 3. Corre. 4. Il mercoledì. 5. Gioca a calcio. 6. Il tennis. 7. Fa molto caldo.

3. 1a; 2c; 3e; 4d; 5b

5. 1. Sulle Alpi nevica e fa molto freddo. 2. A Venezia piove e c'è vento. 3. In Val Padana da Milano a Parma c'è nebbia. 4. A Roma fa discretamente caldo per la stagione. 5. A Bari c'è vento. 6. A Palermo c'è sole e fa piuttosto caldo.

Your turn: Sample answers: 1. Finisco il lavoro alle sei e mezzo la sera, torno a casa, mangio e mi rilasso un po' davanti alla televisione. 2. Mi piace molto il calcio. 3. Lo pratico d'inverno. Faccio l'allenamento il mercoledì sera e spesso c'è una partita il sabato mattina. 4. Vado in vacanza due volte all'anno, in febbraio ed in luglio. 5. In febbraio, vado in montagna qui in Italia ed in luglio vado al mare. Mi piacciono molto le isole greche. 6. Mi piace sciare d'inverno e fare la vela d'estate. 7. Preferisco quando c'è sole e fa caldo ma non troppo caldo.

Extra 1

1. *Sample answers:* Ciao, Stefano, come stai? / Bene, grazie, e tu?; Buona sera, signora Meletti, come sta? / Non sto molto bene.

3. 1d; 2a; 3e; 4f; 5b; 6c

4. chiamo; sono; italiana; è; cognome; dove; abita; questo

Extra 2

1. 1b; 2d; 3a; 4c; 5f; 6e

2. 1. È una storia d'amore molto bella. 2. No, è disoccupato. 3. Beatrice è una bellissima donna che lavora in un bar. 4. Neruda è un poeta. 5. Abita fuori del villaggio e cerca un postino per portare la posta a casa sua. 6. È innamorato di Beatrice. 7. È un uomo semplice e non trova le parole d'amore necessarie. 8. Conquista il cuore di Beatrice.

3. *1. He is unemployed but has a lot of imagination. 2. He works in a large square or in a street where it is possible to park. 3. He helps drivers to find a parking space and looks after the car. 4. If there is no space, the driver leaves the car and the car key with him. 5. Because he is not authorized by the authorities to do it.*

4. *1. It is a selection process (often an exam) for choosing candidates for public office. 2. Every four years at present. 3. Because there are too many teachers at the moment. It is to limit numbers. 4. The Ministry of Education will consider where teachers are needed and will nominate me to a post on that basis.*

Extra 3

1. 1. Mio zio. 2. Mio suocero. 3. Mia cognata. 4. Mio cugino. 5. Mio genero. 6. Mio figlio.

2. 1. Lavora in tivù. 2. Lavora in tivù anche lei. 3. "Solletico" è un programma per bambini. 4. Mara è golosa e divora il cioccolato. 5. È protettiva e severa. 6. Urla come una pazza.

3. 1c; 2d; 3a; 4b

4. Donna 30enne divorziata con una figlia, economicamente indipendente, bella presenza, socievole cerca uomo max 40 anni, dinamico, sportivo e amante del mare.

Extra 4

1. 1. birra; 2. caffè; 3. vino rosso; 4. tè al latte; 5. coca-cola®

2. *The waiter brought a bottle of wine instead of another beer.*

3. *1. It contains maps of the towns, motorways, other roads, and useful information. 2. Extremely up-to-date. 3. An umbrella.*

4. *1. Three. 2. London and England. 3. One chapter on Scotland and one on Wales. 4. Historical notes and useful information.*

Extra 5

1. 1. il Colosseo; 2. il Foro Romano; 3. Piazza Venezia; 4. la fontana di Trevi

2. *1. Basilica di San Pietro. 2. In the Treasures of St. Peter's. 3. One is in white marble, one is in plaster. 4. One is the plaster cast model. 5. It is a splendid golden chapel in the crypt of St. Peter's. 6. In the excavations underneath St. Peter's. 7. Inside the Vatican. The entrance is to the left of the Cathedral. 8. The Swiss Guard.*

Extra 6

1. è; Lavora; Fa; comincia; finisce; arriva; va; Fa; si riposa; esce; incontra; si sente; è; tornano; pranzano; va; comincia; si alza; cena; guarda; ascolta; Esce; fa; beve

2. *Answers will vary.*

Test 1

1. 1. quattro; 2. tre; 3. nove; 4. diciassette; 5. undici; 6. quattordici

2. 1. amico; 2. maschio; 3. sto bene; 4. mi chiamo; 5. quanto; 6. tempo

3. 1. La, il; 2. L', le; 3. Gli, le; 4. Lo; i 5. Il, la; 6. L', il

4. 1. Sono di Milano. 2. Sto benissimo. 3. Trenta. 4. No, è divorziato. 5. Faccio il medico. 6. Per tre mesi.

5. 1. parrucchiera; 2. ingegnere; 3. insegnante; 4. infermiera; 5. avvocato; 6. medico

6. 1. No, sono inglesi. 2. No, è italiano. 3. No, è italiana. 4. No, è americana. 5. No, è americano. 6. No, sono francesi.

7. 1. La sua; 2. Mio; 3. la sua; 4. tuo; 5. la mia; 6. tua

8. 1. Di dov'è ? Di dove sei? 2. Quanti anni ha? Quanti anni hai? 3. È sposata? Sei sposata? 4. Ha figli? Hai figli? 5. Cosa fa? Cosa fai?

9. 1e; 2c; 3f; 4b; 5a; 6d

10. 2, 3, 5, 7

Test 2

1. 1. mattina; 2. insalata; 3. autunno; 4. fragola;
   5. posta; 6. invece

2. 1. È l'una e un quarto di mattina. 2. Sono le dieci e
   mezzo di mattina. 3. È mezzogiorno. 4. Sono le sei
   meno un quarto di sera. 5. Sono le nove meno
   dieci di sera. 6. È mezzanotte.

3. 1. un; 2. un'; 3. un; 4. una; 5. uno; 6. una

4. 1c; 2f; 3d; 4b; 5a; 6e

5. 1. in; 2. a; 3. negli; 4. alla; 5. in; 6. a, al; 7. in; alle

6. 1. prende; 2. preferisco; 3. costa; 4. andiamo; 5. ti
   svegli; 6. litighiamo

7. 1. Cosa prendete? 2. Quanto costano? 3. A che ora
   si alza Marco? 4. Che tempo fa a luglio? 7. Chi è
   Samanta? 6. Dov'è il ristorante?

8. 1. Quando; 2. Dov'è; 3. c'è; 4. costano; 5. Ce n'è;
   6. si sveglia

9. 1. Vorrei un panino. 2. No, grazie, senza. 3. Sì, c'è
   sole e fa caldo. 4. In macchina. 5. Costa 2 euro.

10. 1. maggio; 2. settembre; 3. novembre; 4. gennaio;
    5. luglio; 6. febbraio; 7. ottobre

Notes